The Savvy Client's Guide to
Translation Agencies

How to Find the Right Agency the First Time

John Yunker

Byte Level
Books

www.ByteLevelBooks.com

The Savvy Client's Guide to Translation Agencies
How to Find the Right Agency the First Time

Publisher
Byte Level Books
www.bytelevelbooks.com

ISBN 978-0-9796475-4-3
First Published 2002
Fifth Edition 2010

Contents

Why is the translation industry so hard to understand? 5

Translating the Translation Industry **9**
Talking the Talk: Translation Lingo Demystified 11
Different Content = Different Translation Strategies 19
Understanding the Translation Industry 21
Logistically Speaking: Translation Workflow....................................27
Translation in the Cloud...29
Making Sense of Software 31
A Translator's Point of View: Q&A with Jost Zetzsche 35

Mastering the Multilingual Web..**43**
English as a Second Language..45
What to Know Before Taking Your Web Site Global 48
Spanish for the US 57

Selecting the Right Translation Agency **61**
Ten Things You Should Know About Translation Agencies...............63
Ten Questions to Ask Your Prospective Translation Agency..............68
Translation Costs..73
Reading a Translation Quote...76
Inside the Agency: Q&A with Lionbridge 79
Taking the Mobile App Global: Q&A with Glyph Language Services 86

Agency Directory...**93**
Agencies by Size...95
Agencies by Location 98
Agencies by Specialization 102

Agency Profiles **107**

Acclaro 109

Accuphrase 111

American Translation Partners 113

Argos Translations 115

AST Language Services 117

Ccaps Translation and Localization 119

CPSL (Celer Pawlowsky, SL) 121

CSOFT International 123

E-C Translation 125

Eriksen Translations 127

Globalization Partners International 129

Glyph Language Services 131

Hermes Traducciones y Servicios Lingüísticos 133

HighTech Passport 135

Idea Factory Languages 137

In Every Language 139

InterNation 141

International Language Services (ILS) 143

Jiangsu Sunyu Information Technology Co. 145

Kwintessential 147

Language Connect 149

Lingo24 151

Lingotek 153

Lingua Tech Singapore 155

LinguaLinx Language Solutions 157

Lionbridge Technologies 159

LUZ 161

MAGNUS 163

Matrix Communications 165

Multimedia Languages & Marketing 167

Net-Translators 169

New Market Translations 171

One Hour Translation...173

PTIGlobal...175

Schreiber Translations, Inc. (STI)...177

SDL..179

Syzygy Information Services..181

TransAction Translators...183

Translation Plus..185

TransPerfect Translations International 187

TripleInk...189

Welocalize...191

Wordbank Limited 193

World Language Communications..195

Additional Resources 197

Globalization Checklist..199

Terminology 201

Blogs, Twitter Feeds, and Additional Translation Resources 207

Selected Country Codes..210

Selected Language Codes 211

About the Author...212

Additional Products and Services 213

Why is the translation industry so hard to understand?

Translation doesn't seem to be that complicated—at least initially.

You have something you want translated. A marketing brochure. A web site. A software application. You get on the Internet and you find an agency. You send them the files, and they send you back the translated product. Simple, right?

Not exactly.

For starters, the Internet isn't always the best place to find a translation agency. There are thousands from which to choose, and most will tell you that they offer the highest quality at the lowest price. You could lose a day or two out of your life just surfing through their web sites. That's one reason I wrote this book—to give you a short list of agencies from which to begin. All the key data is cleanly presented, and the agencies are grouped by size, region, and specialty.

But finding an agency is just one of the challenges you'll face. Your product may require a good deal more than translation. You may need localization. Or internationalization. If these terms are new to you, don't worry; you'll know what they mean before you finish this book.

That's the other reason I wrote this book—to help you become a more savvy buyer of translation services. By now I've been both a buyer and provider of translation services for over a decade—but I'll never forget how confused I felt when I first heard terms like "translation memory" and "transcreation."

Over the years, translation agencies have helped companies expand at an amazing pace, adding jobs and creating opportunities. The people who work at these agencies are some of the brightest and culturally adept people you will meet. But for an industry that specializes in multilingual communication, it doesn't always do a good job of translating itself.

This book will help.

The Savvy Client's Guide is designed to be used as both a learning tool and a reference. The first two thirds of the book demystifies the translation industry and its many complex terms and technologies. The last third includes a directory of 44 translation agencies to help you begin your search process.

As has always been our policy, we do not charge agencies to be included in this guide. Nor is this list anything more than a starting point; there are many other agencies to consider. But this guide provides a solid introduction to translation, and we take great pride in offering a directory that is both objective and focused on helping clients make sound buying decisions.

Your translation agency is your voice to the world. Select the right agency, and the world will hear you loud and clear. Select the wrong agency, and the world may never know what you have to say—or worse, hear something you never intended to say. This guide will help you select the right agency the first time.

John Yunker
jyunker@bytelevel.com

Translating the Translation Industry

This section will help you better understand how translation agencies operate, the complex terms and technologies they use, and some key trends now affecting the industry. Please also see the Terminology section at the back of this book for definitions of key terms.

Talking the Talk: Translation Lingo Demystified

You say Translation Agency; they say Language Service Provider

What most clients think of as translation agencies are more commonly referred to, within the industry, as language service providers (LSPs).

Why is this? It's because agencies do a great deal more than translation. It's also because the industry is famous for making things more complicated than they need to be. For example, an LSP may also be known as an SLV or MLV—which stands for single language vendor or multi-language vendor. These terms differentiate between vendors that handle only one language pair (such as a freelance translator) and vendors that handle any number of language pairs.

Translation agencies want to be known, rightly so, for providing much more than translation services. For example, if you have a web site or software application you want translated for the world, what you really want is a localization provider.

Translation vs. Localization

Localization is a term that originated with the software industry. When software (or now a web site or mobile app) is adapted to new markets, it is *localized*—a process that includes both technical and linguistic modifications.

For example, when you localize a web site, you may have to resize user interface elements, such as buttons, message windows, and input forms, to accommodate changing text sizes. When English is translated into German, text may expand by 30% or more. For Asian scripts, the font size usually must be increased by a point or two so the text remains legible.

Localization also requires focusing on region-specific elements, such as currency, date and time formats, and phone numbers. If you use photos of people, you may need to hire local models and align their attire and body language with the target audience. You also have to be sensitive to colors. For example, white, not black, signifies death across much of Asia. When you adapt a web site or marketing brochure or software application for new markets, translation may be the most visible aspect of the process, but it is just one aspect, and sometimes the easiest to accomplish.

Localization, as illustrated below, typically occurs at the end of the development cycle, be it a brochure, a web site, or a piece of software. That is, the product is developed with one language or market in mind and then, after release, the decision is made to localize it for additional markets. The problem with saving localization for last is that you may have designed your product in such a way that it is not easily localized, resulting in significant redesign, rewriting, and re-engineering.

Going global the hard way   **Localization**

| Plan | Develop | Test | Release |

Once a product is released for one market, localizing it
for new markets often requires extensive re-engineering.

For example, if you have an ecommerce web site, you'll need to prepare for multiple address formats, currencies, taxes, and payment options. And your design should be designed so it can easily accomodate a wide range of scripts (Latin, Cyrillic, Chinese, Arabic).

If you wait until the localization stage to tackle these engineering-intensive tasks, you could waste a great deal of time and money.

The best way to minimize localization challenges downstream is to prepare for these challenges as far upstream as possible, ideally during the development process—during a stage known as internationalization.

Internationalization, defined below, is a stage during which the product is made "world ready" well before any localization work is performed.

Going global the smart way

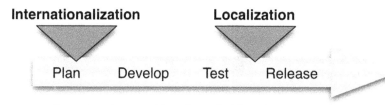

Internationalization   **Localization**

Plan   Develop   Test   Release

By engineering a world-ready product from the beginning, localization is much more efficient.

Internationalization

Internationalization, which also originated in the software industry, is a largely technical process of modifying the software (or web site, app, etc.) so that it can be adapted for any language or market with minimal re-engineering work. Internalization treats English like just another language. In fact, some companies will insert a "pseudo" text that includes a wide mix of languages and scripts to see how the product holds up; this process, known as "pseudolocalization," is used to identify text expansion and display issues as early as possible so they can be addressed by engineers up-stream rather than by localizers further downstream. Internationalization enables you to localize for many languages and markets at the same time and to therefore go global more quickly.

The most important thing to keep in mind is that regardless of what your product is, the earlier you plan for globalization, the fewer problems you will have when you reach the translation stage.

Globalization = Internationalization + Localization

Globalization may be interpreted in many different ways, but for our pur-poses, it includes both internationalization and localization (which natu-rally includes translation). You'll notice here that translation is just one aspect of the localization process.

Internationalization
- Global templates
- Flexible design
- World-ready text
- Global engineering

Localization
- Content
- Formats, measurements, currency, etc.
- Translation

Internationalization and localization complement each other. The better job you do of internationalizing your web site, the fewer problems you'll have when localizing your site for each market.

Many people within this industry resist using the term *globalization* be-cause it can mean so many different things depending on the context. But

I do find that it resonates well when thinking about the overall process of taking anything built for one language or market and adapting it for the world.

i18n and L10n

What are these two strange-looking things? They're not acronyms exactly but "numeronyms." They are used in place of "internationalization" and "localization," respectively—the numbers signify the number of characters they are replacing. These numeronyms are another reason why this industry can be so intimidating to outsiders.

Transcreation

Over the past few years, the concept of *transcreation* has gained in popularity. With translation, the goal is to accurately convey the meaning of the source text into the target text. But what if a literal translation ends up resulting in text that is not effective?

If you're translating instructions for how to use a medical device, a literal translation is desirable. That is, you don't want the translator to "get creative."

However, if you're translating marketing copy for a new brand of potato chip, you may very well want the translator to take some creative license. Taglines are particularly difficult to translate literally. For example, years ago Dell wanted to translate its slogan "Easy as Dell" for Japan. A literal translation didn't make much sense to users, so the slogan was transcreated to mean "Simple for you, Dell," which appealed to the local market. This may sound like a minor adjustment, but a great deal of effort went into it. Nike tried to translate "Just do it" globally but ultimately gave up. Not everything will translate well for the world.

Translation memory

This term causes a good deal of head scratching among first-time clients. The term really means translation "re-use." That is, once you've translated a sentence or text string, you should be able to re-use that translation if you encounter a similar text string at a later point. To re-use translation, you need translation memory software—the leader being SDL Trados. Translators will use this software as they translate and, as repeated strings are encountered, they simply re-use the translation, saving time and the client's money.

As the translation memory (TM) grows in size, it becomes increasingly valuable for cutting translation costs as well as increasing consistency. In addition, specialized terminology memories can be developed to ensure that a "dual overhead cam," for instance, is consistently translated throughout an auto repair manual.

But be aware that translation memories don't become valuable until they have grown to include many thousands of translated text pairs. And even then, you need your source text to be consistent so that there are increased odds of repeated text strings. For example, if your writers keep changing their writing style, or if you use many different writers, the value of translation memories may decrease.

As you begin your translation efforts, building a translation memory may not be very important. And you may not bother building a memory until you have several projects completed. That said, companies that translate more than 100,000 words are wise to investigate the use of translation memories. Just be sure that your agency puts in writing that whatever memories are created remain the property of the client. Some translation vendors have been known to retain the translation memories as a means of retaining clients.

Machine translation

Machine translation (MT) is a term that originated back when computers were known as machines. Back then, it was thought that computers would replace human translators "any day now."

Clearly, that hasn't happened. But over the past decade a more advanced type of machine translation has emerged, spearheaded most successfully by Google.

You may be well acquainted with the Google Translate interface, shown here, but Google has also integrated this engine into many applications, such as Gmail and the Chrome web browser. Today, Google Translate handles more translation per day than all the human translators in the world handle in a year.

Known as statistical machine translation (SMT), Google's technology relies on algorithms and brute-force computing to "learn" as it processes more and more text. Companies such as Microsoft, HP, Intel, and Cisco all use machine translation in varying capacities. Some companies use MT only internally, to translate communications between different offices around the world, as well as to get the gist of news reports in different countries. Some companies use MT as a first pass of translation workflow. And a few companies have used MT as a stand-alone solution, as Microsoft has done with parts of its knowledgebase. The thing to keep in mind about machine translation is that it has a valuable role to play within many companies, translating content that would be too expensive to translate by humans, or helping translators do their work more quickly. And this role is sure to grow in the years ahead.

As for the name itself, many vendors are trying to move away from "machine translation" to terms like "automated translation" or "real-time translation" in order to make the terminology sound more up-to-date.

FIGS, CJK, and BRIC

Brace yourself for acronyms. Translation agencies use a number of acronyms for languages and countries, such as FIGS (French, Italian, German, Spanish), CJK (Chinese, Japanese, Korean), and BRIC (Brazil, Russia, India, China). You may also see FIGSP (FIGS + Portuguese), but be sure to clarify between Portuguese for Brazil vs. Portuguese for Portugal.

You'll also see arrows "<>" used to denote source and target language, such as "English > French" which means English translated into French. If your agency uses an acronym or symbol that you don't fully understand, don't hesitate to ask what it means.

Different Content = Different Translation Strategies

You cannot afford to translate everything you want to translate.

No company can.

But that doesn't mean most or all of your content can't be made available to users in their native language. The key is to understand what content must be translated by humans and what content can be translated by more automated means.

As shown below, a company may develop different translation strategies for different types of content.

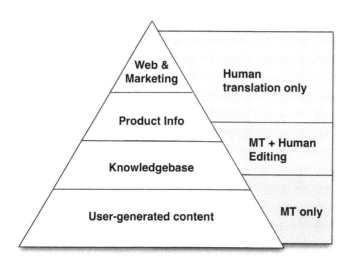

Naturally, the text that is most mission critical is translated by professional translators. But as the perceived value of the content decreases, and the quantity of content increases, the only way to make it available to users is to find a machine translation solution.

Check your web logs. It's quite possible that many of your customers around the world have automatically translated parts of your web site using machine translation from Microsoft or Google. Instead of forcing your customers and visitors to self-translate with highly variable results, you can use machine translation internally, customized to your company's terminology, to produce a higher quality level of content.

Microsoft, for example, has used machine translation to provide its knowledgebase in both Japanese and Spanish, without using human translators. Microsoft clearly labels this content as machine translated, so users know what to expect, but the company reports very positive user experiences. And Microsoft is no longer alone in using MT to help translate content that is simply too expensive to translate by hand.

Understanding the Translation Industry

If you understand in broad terms how the translation industry operates, its major players, and its standard operating practices, you'll be in a much better position as you begin soliciting requests for information. This section will get you started.

Translation is largely a "mom and pop" industry

There are anywhere between 3,000 and 6,000 translation agencies around the world, 99% of which employ fewer than three people and bring in less than $150,000 a year in revenues. Why so many small shops? Because the translation industry has very low barriers to entry—any freelance translator can become an "agency" by setting up a web site and taking orders. In fact, many of the larger translation firms competing today were started by freelance translators who gradually expanded their businesses to include a greater number of language pairs.

With so many small firms competing against one another, price wars are frequent and sometimes quite ruthless. At industry gatherings, often the chief complaint I hear is that translation vendors have become their own worst enemies. And in many respects, I agree. As a profession, the translation industry has no standardized system of accreditation or oversight. Individual translators may be accredited by the American Translators Association (www.atanet.org), but many choose not to participate. There is no such program available for agencies, so clients are often left wondering if the agency they've selected will produce quality work.

Yet as a buyer of translation services, you shouldn't assume that smaller agencies are any less qualified than larger agencies. In fact, many small agencies are small by choice and have client relationships that have lasted 20 years or longer. But given the wide range of agencies from which to choose, you should invest the time upfront to make sure that your agency is going to be a good fit now and well into the future.

Most translation is outsourced (and that's okay)

The major challenge translation agencies face is managing sudden spikes in both volume of words and breadth of languages. Even the very large agencies, those with numerous in-house translators, will outsource translation to freelance translators. The agencies maintain a roster of freelance translators and smaller translation agencies that they can reliably work with.

Outsourced translation is not something to be feared. In fact, the outsourcing model allows agencies to pair your content with the best qualified translators— those who are experts in your terminology as well as experts in your target market. The outsourcing process is generally a transparent affair; clients often play an active role in selecting the translators with whom they wish to work.

Many clients work with multiple agencies

If you're just getting started with translation, one agency will probably suffice. But if you've got large volumes of localization work or a diverse range of products to be localized (software, web sites, brochures), then it makes sense to retain more than one vendor. Doing so gives you peace of mind in case one vendor can't handle a sudden spike in volume, or a particular type of localization project. You also will benefit from having two or more trusted vendors on hand that you can bid jobs out to without having to go through a full RFP process.

Many agencies overpromise

Because the industry is so competitive, many agencies will say they are experts at literally everything to win a job—from translating product instructions for complex medical devices to localizing iPhone apps. And, in some cases, agencies are well positioned to work across a wide range of industries and project types, particularly the larger agencies. Just be aware that you have to conduct due diligence to be sure that your prospective agency truly can handle everything it says it can. As a general rule, the more specialized your particular industry and terminology are, the more carefully you should proceed before selecting a translation partner. Fortunately, a number of agencies have specialized over the years along certain industries, which I highlight in the Agency Directory section of this book.

What's your word count?

If you need to translate a business card, most agencies aren't going to be too excited to get your business. Why? Because agencies typically charge by source word count, multiplied by the number of target languages. A business card with a few source words translated into just one language, from an agency's perspective, is hardly worth quoting.

However, if you've got a 200-page instruction manual that you need translated into six languages, you'll have agencies banging at your door for an opportunity to quote. That manual could easily be a $50,000 job. Agencies love long documents and software products that must be translated into more than one language, and they will devote the bulk of their energies targeting those accounts.

Because word count is the foundation for quoting prices, you are wise to do all you can to keep your word count to a minimum. As a client, your first priority is to ask, "Is this text worth translating?" Extra editing before you begin soliciting translation quotes can go a long way toward saving many thousands of dollars down the road.

Some agencies also offer editing services to help clients cut down the word count of the source content. At a penny or two per word, this service can indeed add up to significant savings down the road. In translation, less is more.

Beware of change orders

Let's say you've sent your marketing brochure to the translation agency and the next day your CEO wants to change a few sentences in that brochure. Naturally, you'll have to "halt the presses" with your agency, but if work has already begun, you may be hit with a change order. Change orders are how agencies get compensated for any change of project scope. We've witnessed several agency/client relationships go sour because there was not a clear understanding of what type of change in scope resulted in what type of expense.

Change orders may be trivial if you only encounter a few a year. The key lesson here is to "freeze" your source content before sending it to your translation agency. And also be clear on what the costs will be if change orders are incurred. You can then make sure your colleagues are aware of the costs before they approve any changes.

Did a human translate this—or a computer?

Given the increased quality of certain machine translation applications—particularly when customized per industry—some translators will use machine translation for the initial translation. Their role switches to one of "post editing."

This scenario is attractive because it can greatly accelerate turnaround and reduce costs. And it opens vast new quantities of content for translation that might have been too expensive to translate under the old model of translator, editor, proofreader.

But machine translation is no panacea. Consistently written source text is required to ensure high-quality output, and the tools themselves require a great deal of customization before they can begin to replace a human translator.

As a buyer of translation, you should study MT and begin thinking about how it might benefit your business. MT is going to dramatically change the translation industry—for the better—in the years ahead.

Keep control of your translation memories

Years ago, many translation agencies used the translation memories they had developed for their clients as leverage to keep their clients from jumping ship. This practice has mostly faded thanks to client pressure, but, as mentioned previously, be sure you have in writing that all translation memories that an agency develops while working for you shall be your property and will be delivered to you after the completion of all major projects. Because of the cost savings, translation memories, like bank accounts, can grow in value over time.

Your translation agency isn't just your global voice but also your eyes and ears

Translation agencies not only will help you communicate with the world, they can also help you understand how the world views your company, products, and your content. Some of this feedback will happen quite naturally, as project managers and translators review the content. Some companies will hire agencies specifically for cultural consulting prior to content creation.

The project managers you work with will, over time, become extensions of your company; they will become experts on your products and your terminology. In some cases, for large accounts, these project managers actually work out of their clients' offices.

Despite all the advances of translation workflow technology, it is the people who manage their technology who matter most. Invest the time getting to know these people and how they work, think, and will mesh with your work environment.

Logistically Speaking: Translation Workflow

Successful translation projects depend on skilled linguists and project managers. While the linguist do the translating and editing, the project managers (PMs) make sure everything moves quickly, smoothly, and with minimal room for error. Below are the essential steps for translating a file from one language into another.

1. Client prepares the file for translation, including a terminology glossary and detailed instructions.
2. File is sent to translation agency project manager (PM).
3. PM sends file to translator.
4. Translator returns completed file to PM, along with generated translation memories (if required).
5. PM sends file to editor.
6. Editor returns completed file to PM.
7. PM makes final edits and returns file to client.

A good agency will rely on at least two linguists for every project—the translator and an editor. The translator takes the first pass at the project, then the editor (who typically has more translation and industry experience) makes any necessary final changes. Editors are important for checking style, consistency, and proper use of terminology. Sometimes an additional proofreader is also employed, particularly with mission-critical translations.

It's important to have a project manager who understands how to manage deadlines and to properly communicate instructions and changes between the linguists and the client. Along the way, there are usually queries from both translator and editor that the client may be required to answer.

A lot of work and a lot of flow

At a minimum, each language will require a project manager and two linguists. Multiply that by a 20-language project and you've got at least 40 people involved, all sending files back and forth.

Basic Translation Workflow

For years, translation of files meant juggling files between many people. Each additional language required additional players and complexity.

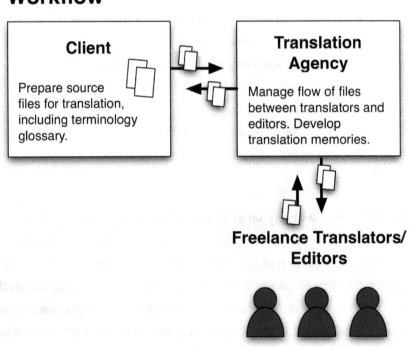

Client

Prepare source files for translation, including terminology glossary.

Translation Agency

Manage flow of files between translators and editors. Develop translation memories.

Freelance Translators/ Editors

Translation in the Cloud

An increasing number of companies are hosting their translateable content on a shared web server (the "cloud") so the content creators, project managers, and translators all work from a common platform. Needless to say, a cloud-based model of translation cuts down on the emailing of files. As shown below, the content to be translated is uploaded to a shared portals and all the participants do their work online. As a client, this model gives you a real-time view of progress being made on your project.

Cloud-based Translation Workflow

A centralized location enables faster workflow and the sharing of translation memories in real time.

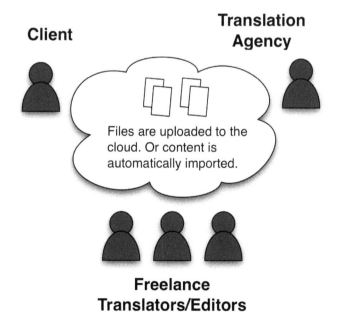

Client

Translation Agency

Files are uploaded to the cloud. Or content is automatically imported.

Freelance Translators/Editors

In the Agency Profiles section of this book, we asked each agency what percentage of their work is done "in the cloud." You can use this data as a starting point should you wish to adopt this workflow.

Keep in mind, however, that the cloud may not work for everyone. Some clients would rather not have their content shared on an external server. Others have developed their own internal workflows that they would rather their agencies use. But it's safe to say that the trend is toward variations on this model. The more busywork you can remove from the translation workflow, the faster the turnaround and the lower the overall costs.

Making Sense of Software

One of the more intimidating aspects of the content globalization industry are the tools unique to the industry. This section provides a high-level view of the major tools used within the industry and how they are used.

Keep In Mind...

While tools are often an invaluable part of successful translation and web globalization projects, they are by no means a panacea. Every tool presents unique integration and learning challenges and may not always be the best solution for a given project. Sometimes tools create more problems than they solve.

In general, the tools presented here are designed to assist or automate the following activities:

- **Translation management** (including translation memory and terminology management)
- **Content authoring and editing**
- **Global content management**
- **Machine translation** (real-time translation/automated translation)

Translation Management Software

While translation is fundamentally a human endeavor, computers play an important role in both accelerating translation and enabling more consistent translation. As mentioned previously, translation memories play an important role in helping companies re-use previous translation. Of course, translators need software to help them create and leverage translation memories, which is why the "translation software management" category evolved. For years, SDL Trados has been the most commonly used tool within this category, and thousands of translators and translation agencies currently support it.

But the rise of cloud computing and new vendors is breathing new life into this software category. For example, Lionbridge offers a web-based translation portal for its customers as well as a fee-based service for other agencies and clients known as GeoWorkz. MadCap Lingo provides a popular software suite that combines content authoring and translation memory in a user-friendly package. And Wordbee and Web Translate It are two web-based-only platforms.

As a client, it's important to study the following vendors and their products so that you get a feel for the different approaches to successful translation management. There isn't just one right way to manage translation.

- SDL Trados — www.sdl.com
- Lionbridge Translation Workspace — www.lionbridge.com
- Déjà Vu — www.atril.com
- memoQ — www.kilgray.com
- STAR Transit — www.star-group.net
- Wordbee — www.wordbee.com
- Wordfast — www.wordfast.net
- MadCap Lingo — www.madcapsoftware.com
- Web Translate It — webtranslateit.com

Content Management Systems (CMS) and Globalization Management Systems (GMS)

Enterprises have long relied on content management systems to manage documents and web sites both internally and externally. The benefit of CMS tools is that they often enable non-technical people to create and manage content on web sites and throughout the enterprise. Most CMS packages today will support the publishing and management of multiple languages, even the more complex double-byte character sets used in Asian languages. However, not all CMS tools provide support for globalization workflow; this is where the globalization management system comes into play. The line between CMS and GMS tools has blurred as clients demand fully integrated software solutions.

Selecting a CMS or GMS package is one of the most important (and potentially expensive) decisions a company can make regarding its global content. The list of software vendors below is by no means comprehensive, and there has been significant consolidation over the past few years, such as SDL purchasing Idiom and Open Text purchasing RedDot. But the most disruptive developments in this space has been the rise of open-source solutions, such as Joomla for CMS and GlobalSight for translation workflow management. I advise evaluating all options before you dive in.

- Autonomy   www.autonomy.com
- Open Text   www.opentext.com
- SDL WorldServer   www.sdl.com
- Ektron   www.ektron.com
- XTM Suite   www.xtm-intl.com
- Joomla   www.joomla.org
- GlobalSight   www.globalsight.com

Software Localization Tools

Localizing software is no trivial task. Text strings may be scattered across a wide variety of file types and embedded deep within complex binary code. Over the years, software tools have been developed that help translators effectively isolate, translate, and re-use translated text. Here are three popular tools:

- SDL Passolo   www.passolo.com
- Alchemy CATALYST   www.alchemysoftware.ie
- Lingobit   www.lingobit.com

Machine Translation (MT) Tools

While Google Translate is probably the MT tool you are most familiar with, it is by no means the only MT tool. The challenge with MT is integrating it into your translation workflow and refining it so that the quality improves based on your terminology and audience. The challenge with Google and Microsoft is that their MT engines are not easily adapted to corporate translation workflows. Systran and SDL's BeGlobal are engines that companies can in fact adapt to their needs. And Moses is unique in that it is fully open source.

- Bing (Microsoft) Translator   translate.bing.com
- Google Translate   translate.google.com
- SDL BeGlobal   www.sdl.com
- Systran   www.systran.com
- ProMT   www.promt.com
- Asia Online   www.asiaonline.net
- Moses   www.statmt.org/moses

A Translator's Point of View: Q&A with Jost Zetzsche

Jost Zetzsche is an English-into-German translator, a localization and translation consultant, and a widely published author of books and articles on technical aspects of translation. He also publishes the very popular newsletter *The Translator's Tool Kit*. A native of Hamburg, Germany, he earned a Ph.D. in the field of Chinese translation history and linguistics, and began working in localization and technical translation in 1997. In 1999, he co-founded International Writers' Group (www.international-writers.com) on the Oregon coast.

What is your general output of translation and/or editing in terms of words per day?

My output depends on a number of things: first and foremost, how familiar I am with the subject matter; and second, what kind of assets I have that help me with my translation. These assets include translation memories, terminology databases, and access to third-party resources. So, if everything goes well, I translate about 5,000 words a day; if I have to do a lot of footwork, it can be as low as 1,500 words.

What software tools do you typically use for translation?

My main tool is a computer-aided translation tool or, as I like to call it, a translation environment tool. I have access to a number of different translation environment tools, but if possible I like to use the same tool for most projects—this way I have easy access to my resources without having to go through conversions, which in almost all cases come with some loss of data integrity. In addition, since the different vendors of translation environment tools have not yet found a standard to exchange the different sets of keyboard shortcuts, my "finger memory" also makes me prefer to stay with one tool.

Other tools that I use include tools that allow me to quickly access online- and hard-drive-based linguistic resources, advanced text editors for dealing with code page conversion issues, Acrobat for proofreading purposes (many clients send PDFs for a final proof run), speech-recognition software for dictation, and various desktop publishing and office programs.

Do you prefer to work with clients directly or through translation agencies? And why?

The easy answer is that I prefer to deal directly with end-clients because this typically allows me to charge more, to account for my own overhead (file prep work, project management, etc.). But I also value relationships that I have with translation agencies, especially when the project manager that I'm dealing with is skilled and prepares projects in a way that allows me to focus on the linguistic aspects of the job.

Clients are generally advised to use translators who live in the target market. But in this virtually connected world we live in, how relevant is that advice today?

There is value in using translators in the target market—but I also see value in using translators in the source market, especially when it results in a more profound understanding of the source text. Either way, you're right in assuming that a virtually connected world makes these boundaries increasingly unimportant. Anything from web-based resources to radio and other media to free or inexpensive VoIP services blurs the differences in where you live.

Have you ever said "no" to accepting a translation project? If so, why?

Goodness, yes—many times. The most obvious reason is that I'm often overbooked, but I also, and often, reject projects because I lack experience in the subject matter.

In addition, clients often get my language combination (English-into-German) confused and send me German-into-English projects, which I do not work on.

Are there times when you suggest that clients rewrite the source text before translation?

Yes, but it is very rare for a client to heed that advice. In fact, it's more likely that I end up rejecting a job if the text is so badly written that translation is virtually impossible. Of course, any text (and any translation) has minor problems here and there, and part of the assignment of the translator is to point these out to the client. If, however, the problems are so ubiquitous that it would take as much time to point out specific problems as to translate, and the translation project is still a go, the client will receive a general review of the source text quality rather than a specific account.

What types of questions should companies ask when selecting individual translators and editors to work on their projects?

Aside from the correct language combination and the general translation competency, companies should ask about the specific subject matter knowledge. As a client, I would be cautious of translators and editors who claim to have "general expertise." Unless the client can offer excellent translation memories, terminology databases, and other assets to support the translator, the success of the project rises and falls with the subject matter expertise of the translator.

Another area that the client needs to evaluate is whether translators are equipped to deal with the technical aspects of the job. Can they work with XML or other complex file formats? Do they understand issues with code pages and possible conversions? Can they work with binary executables? Almost every job has its own set of technical challenges that the translator will have to be able to meet.

What are some of the most common mistakes that clients make when sending files out to be translated for the first time?

The most common mistake I can think of is that clients actually don't send them out. This is especially true when it comes to smaller web sites. Some clients assume that the translator will be able to somehow download the web pages and translate those. While it's possible to download the web pages, this is not what the client wants to have translated, certainly not for dynamic, database- or CMS-driven websites, but also not for static web-sites. Translators will need to work with the original source files, whether they are multimedia or text-based files.

The other problem is PDF files, which are inherently difficult to translate. While there are many ways to convert PDF files to a translatable format, none of these methods works without loss, and all of them create a lot of overhead work. Of course, the same is true for other binary formats in which text cannot be processed, including multimedia files. In all of these cases, both the client and the translator fare much better if the original source files can be used (for example, a Photoshop .psd file rather than a

.gif file or an InDesign or FrameMaker file rather than a PDF).

If clients use translation environment tools such as Trados, memoQ, or Star Transit, it's helpful to receive the files in a (exchange) format that can also be processed by competing tools so that the translator can utilize his or her own assets for the translation process.

Quality can be difficult to measure. How do you recommend clients measure translation quality?

The 64,000-thousand-dollar question! This question is probably as old as translation itself. There have been many attempts to answer it, but so far no satisfactory answer has been found that can be applied universally. Ironically, the machine translation community has come closer to finding an answer to this than anyone else by switching the concept of "quality" with "usability." According to this concept, if a translation is usable in a given context and for a given audience, it's a successful translation. This usability yardstick could apply equally to a machine-translated knowledge-based article that jars the heart of the language lover but satisfies its goal of communicating to users about how to reboot their computers as well as to an expensive ad campaign for a new market by a large team of translators and marketing specialists.

In more practical terms, any client would be well advised to use a workflow that ensures a certain level of control and accountability of translator and editor. This could include an in-country review, a sampling of the translation by a third party or, to stick with the above-mentioned usability criterion, the end user.

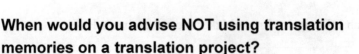

When would you advise NOT using translation memories on a translation project?

The standard answer here is for literary projects and extremely creative texts such as advertisements, but I'm not sure that this is actually true. In those extreme examples, the translation memory paradigm of perfect and fuzzy matches will not be useful, but the translation memory can still serve as a helpful resource when it comes to looking up terms and phrases in context in other occurrences. And it's important to remember that translation memory functionality never comes on its own. It's always part of a translation environment tool that offers a wide range of other features, including terminology management, quality assurance, the ability to work in complex file formats, etc. In addition, while it is often said that translation environment tools limit creativity because of their segmentation (typically on a sentence-by-sentence basis), this also depends on the translator's ability to work with his or her tool: many texts that I translate I segment only on a paragraph level.

So, the short answer is this: I can't remember the last time I did not use a translation environment tool for a project.

Do you use machine translation in your projects? And what are your thoughts about MT in general?

No, I don't use machine translation in my projects, but it's not out of principle—I simply have not found it useful so far. I do think that our profession is at the brink of starting to use MT—many translators already do, and virtually all tools today have some kind of link-in to some of the free online MT systems such as Google Translate or the Microsoft Bing Translator. I think that the most hopeful development for individual translators is represented by the latest versions of machine translation systems like ProMT or Systran. While these systems are rule-based, they now also

40

allow for processing the user's previous translation data to receive better results. For larger translation providers, the open-source Moses engine is particularly interesting.

In general, translators who are traditionally very skeptical of machine translation should be eager to leverage the great surge right now in the public's interest in machine translation as an opportunity to talk about the various kinds of translations: from the kind where machine translation will play (and is already playing) a role, to the many other kinds where human involvement or only mere human effort is necessary. This is a real opportunity for us.

Mastering the Multilingual Web

This section provides key data and best practices for developing multilingual web sites—and for understanding how web browsers can "request" content in different languages.

English as a Second Language

English may be the primary language companies use on their global web sites, but it is increasingly just one of many languages used on web sites. That's because the demographics of web users have changed dramatically over the past decade.

No longer is English the dominant language of web users. The Internet now connects two billion people around the world. Most of these Internet users do not live in the United States. And most do not speak English as a native language.

Languages of Internet Users 2010

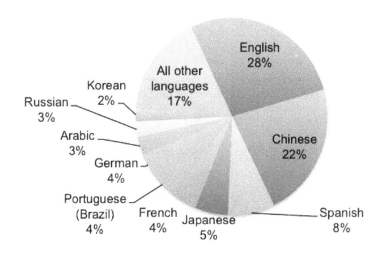

Source: Internet World Stats

Every year, an additional 100 million people go online for the very first time, most of whom also do not live in the US or speak English.

Not surprisingly, companies have responded to the changing mix of Internet users by localizing their web sites and marketing materials.

As noted in my report *The 2010 Web Globalization Report Card*, the average number of languages supported by large multinationals is now 20, up from 12 just five years ago.

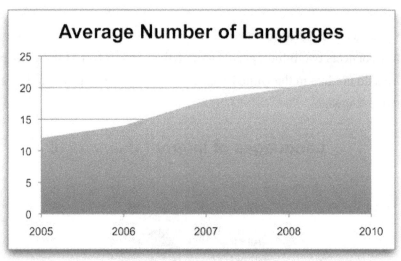

2010 Web Globalization Report Card | www.bytelevel.com

And this is just the average number of languages. Apple, for example, has doubled the number of languages it supports on its web site over the past three years, to 24 today. And Facebook exploded from two languages to more than 70 in less than two years.

As shown here, six different companies across six different industries have all experienced language growth over the past three years. And because so many people within a company contribute to web sites—from marketing to customer support—it's vital that everyone within the company understand general web globalization best practices.

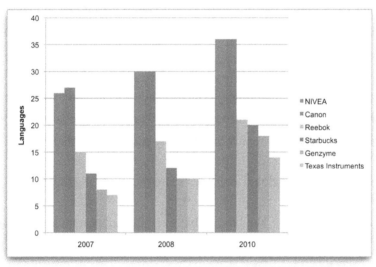

2010 Web Globalization Report Card | www.bytelevel.com

What to Know Before Taking Your Web Site Global

Of the 44 translation agencies included in this guide, more than half reported that web globalization activity is booming. Companies need their web sites localized so they can expand into new markets and broaden their customer base within existing markets. And those companies that already have localized web sites continue to expand into new markets and new languages.

For newcomers, web globalization can be a painful and expensive cycle of trial and error. This section introduces a number of web globalization best practices to help your company build a truly successful global web site.

I have found that best global web sites share the following attributes:

- GLOBAL REACH: The best global web sites support an average of 40 languages, which allow them to communicate with more than 95% of all Internet users.
- GLOBAL GATEWAY: The localized web sites are easy to find, regardless of the user's language.
- GLOBALIZATION: Web design and branding is globally consistent across all local sites, but still flexible enough to support local content and features.
- LOCALIZATION: The content (visuals, text, functionality) are fully localized for the user's country and culture.
- COMMUNITY LOCALIZATION: Content is sourced and/or translated locally via community and social networking platforms.

Every year, I evaluate more than 200 web sites according to these attributes. Based on our most recent analysis, here are some of the best sites overall, representing a wide array of industries:

- Google
- Facebook
- Cisco Systems
- Philips
- Samsung
- 3M
- Caterpillar
- Deloitte Touche Tohmatsu
- Volvo Cars
- Hotels.com
- IKEA
- Adidas

While no web site is perfect, these sites stand apart for their success in implementing the five key attributes mentioned above. Take the time to study them so that you can hit the ground running with your web site.

Set Realistic, Reachable Goals

Google didn't emerge as a 120-language search engine overnight; it began as an English-language search engine that steadily added support for more and more languages. I recommend that companies that are new to web globalization begin with just one language and grow from there. US-based companies generally begin with Spanish, as this is not a technically challenging language and because most companies have Spanish-speaking employees who can assist with language reviews. Be aware that languages based on non-Latin scripts, such as Japanese, Russian, and Arabic, pose much greater challenges. Spanish is a good language to begin with to help you get your workflow running smoothly.

Whether you begin with one language or six languages, mistakes are inevitable. By starting small, you conserve resources and learn important lessons that you can apply to all subsequent web sites.

Also, you will probably want your first localized site to be a subset of your source language web site. After all, you probably won't want to translate such items as "help wanted" pages and pages for products that aren't sold in a given market.

Develop a tiered globalization strategy

Web globalization is a zero-sum game. Because companies only have so much money to allocate to web globalization, they tend to devote more resources to larger "strategic" markets than to smaller markets. This means that not all country web sites will get the same degree of support, which can lead to friction internally and unhappy customers externally.

To ensure that companies successfully align their web globalization objectives with their budgets, I recommend developing a tiered web globalization strategy. This approach begins with the understanding that not all country web sites will get the same financial support but that even the lowest tiers of web globalization, if managed well, can create a positive user experience.

A tiered strategy is best illustrated by a matrix, as shown here.

	Company info translation	Depth of product description translation	Native-language phone support	Native-language email support	Localized ecommerce (pricing, shipping, tariffs)
Tier 1	100%	90%	Yes	Yes	Yes
Tier 2	100%	50%	No	Yes	Yes
Tier 3	100%	25%	No	No	No

A company may give "tier 1" support to its US site while giving "tier 2" support to strategic markets (i.e., Japan, Germany, UK) and "tier 3" support to markets in which it wishes to begin testing without investing too heavily. The bottom tier may not have full e-commerce support, but it still may provide some degree of information and support to the customer or prospect.

Finally, determine what metrics you will use to measure the success of the new web site. We recommend looking beyond traffic measurements to direct sales and lead generation. These metrics will go a long way in getting upper management and in-country sales teams excited about the possibilities of the local web site.

Managing user expectations

The key to a successful tiered strategy is not under-investing in markets to the extent to which customers have a negative experience. You always have to be mindful of the user and what the user expects in order to generate a positive shopping experience. Ask yourself: What is the minimum our web sites need to do to create a positive user experience? And then work up from there. The tiered approach allows retailers to test market opportunities before opening stores within a given market.

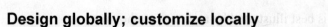

Design globally; customize locally

Once you begin planning your global web site, consider developing a global template. The best web sites (see the IKEA example below) apply a global design template across all country and language sites. A global template need not prevent country offices from having plenty of room for localization. In fact, the very best global tem plates allocate more than 75% of the screen real estate for local promotions.

The IKEA template shown here conveys a consistent brand image and navigation system while allowing the local sites room enough to develop their own content and promotions.

Germany

Japan

Develop a global gateway strategy

You cannot be sure that every visitor to your site enters through the "front door" of your .com home page. For example, a search engine may take users directly to a product or support page; once there, if people cannot easily locate their language or country web site, sales may be lost.

To gracefully accommodate all users, web sites may rely on up to four overlapping devices that collectively form a global gateway. A global gateway is much more than a pull-down menu. It is an umbrella term for the visual and technical elements you employ to direct users to their locale- and language-specific web sites. The four main elements are:

- COUNTRY CODE TOP-LEVEL DOMAIN (ccTLD): Such as .fr for France and .de for Germany
- SPLASH GLOBAL GATEWAY: A landing navigation page for first-time visitors
- PERMANENT GLOBAL GATEWAY: A navigation element that is highly visible on all web pages
- LANGUAGE NEGOTIATION & GEOLOCATION: Behind-the-scenes technologies for detecting the user's location and language preference

If you can use only one gateway element, use the permanent global gateway. This ensures that no matter where users are on your web site, they can find their way to their country and/or language.

Notice the permanent gateway, circled, in the upper right corner of the Caterpillar Japan page:

The map icon makes it clear to those who may not understand Japanese that if they click it they're likely to find their native language—or at least a different language. And when they select this link, they are taken to this page:

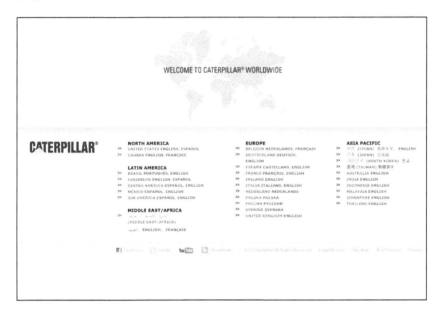

This gateway does two things quite nicely:

o The local links are provided in the end user's language.
o The gateway does not exhibit preference for any one country or region.

Understanding geolocation and language negotiation

If you've used Google, you're probably already familiar with geolocation. Geolocation is what works behind the scenes to serve local ads to the right of your search results. Or, if you're traveling in another country and look up Google.com, geolocation may result in you visiting a Google home page in a different language. Geolocation is the process of looking at a computer's IP address (or a mobile phone's latitude/longitude coordinates) and responding with local content.

Geolocation is becoming more and more popular, but it should never be used instead of a visual global gateway. This is because geolocation is not 100% perfect. For those who do travel a lot, geolocation often leads to many incorrect assumptions about what language they speak.

Language negotiation is another backend technology, in which the web server looks at the language preference of the user's web browser and responds with matching content (if available). Language negotiation is used heavily by Google (and Facebook).

The most important thing to keep in mind about backend technologies is that they should not fully replace visual global gateways. Visual gateways ensure that web users can override server settings in case it guesses incorrectly.

For more tips on global gateways, see *The Art of the Global Gateway* (www.bytelevel.com/books/gateway).

Spanish for the US

According to the US Census, in 2008 there were more than 48 million Hispanics living in the US. In 2050, the population is project to exceed 132 million.

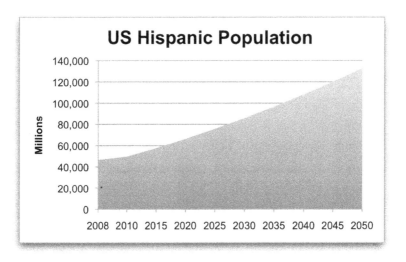

If the US Hispanic population were viewed as a country onto itself, it would be second in size only to Mexico. Not surprisingly, many US companies have responded with Spanish-language advertising, signage, and web sites, including:

- Citibank
- CNN
- Coca-Cola
- MySpace
- PayPal

- Toyota
- Yahoo!

But just as English usage and spelling rules vary around the world, so does Spanish. Companies tend to focus on translating into the Spanish used by Mexicans, but this strategy isn't perfect. If you are focused on reaching Spanish speakers in the New York area or South Florida, you'll likely want to pursue a different flavor of Spanish. Or, better yet, you may want to use a "universal" Spanish.

Understanding "Universal" Spanish

Universal Spanish is an attempt by companies to create a "one size fits all" language that works across all Spanish speakers, whether they are from Mexico, Puerto Rico, or Spain. Think of it as a more generic form of the language, in which specific cultural or regional references are avoided.

Keep in mind, however, that the more generic the language, the less powerful it can potentially become. While a more generic language is probably not an issue with product documentation, it could have a negative impact on marketing text.

A number of agencies listed in this book have experience developing universal Spanish. You'll want to rely on Spanish linguists that know what words to avoid and, more important, can ensure that your "universal" translation is still going to be effective with your target audience.

Selecting the Right Translation Agency

With so many translation agencies from which to choose, how do you choose the right one? This section includes questions you should ask of any potential agency as well as insights into a few agencies.

Ten Things You Should Know About Translation Agencies

By understanding how an agency operates, you are in a stronger position to negotiate the best rates and will be more likely to forge a strong, long-lasting partnership with that agency.

Here are 10 things to keep in mind:

1. Most translation is outsourced

Even the largest translation firms—with hundreds of in-house translators—regularly depend on a global network of freelance translators. Why? Because it is generally not economical to hire full-time translators to manage all the possible language pairs at all times. Translation workflow can be highly erratic and unpredictable, and cost control is essential for survival. In fact, you will notice in the Agency Profiles section that many smaller agencies reference some of the largest agencies as clients.

Looking ahead, the outsourcing trend is sure to accelerate. Agencies are growing more sophisticated at leveraging currency exchange rates and capitalizing on workers in less-developed markets to get more bang for their buck. And as companies ask for a wider range of languages, agencies will seek out translators skilled in those languages. Outsourcing does not necessarily result in lower-quality translation; it is simply a fact of the industry. However, as a client, it is important to fully understand who is going to be translating your text. Many clients play an active role in evaluating translator credentials before work begins.

2. Agencies crave volume and predictability

If an agency charges a client by the number of words to be translated, the agency will naturally be seeking out the types of clients and jobs that result in high-word-count and recurring projects. What if your project meets neither of these criteria? Look for a smaller agency, one that will be happy to have the job.

3. An agency that can translate a document into 100 languages may not be any more qualified than an agency that can manage only 10 languages

There are several thousand languages in existence, yet most companies rarely need translation for more than 30 languages. In fact, few web sites support more than 30 languages. Since most translation is outsourced to freelancers, the number of languages an agency claims, is, to a large degree, irrelevant. Many agencies believe that they will win more business if they claim to support more languages.

4. The fewer translators, the better

If you have a $25,000 translation project that you need completed in three days, you'll have no trouble finding agencies happy to take on the job. But that doesn't mean you'll be getting the best-quality translation. After all, translation is a human endeavor, and humans can only work so quickly. If a project is large and must be completed under tight deadlines, it will be chopped up into pieces and farmed out to dozens of translators.

Suddenly, the room for error grows considerably larger, and overall writing style and tone lose all consistency. Sometimes deadlines simply cannot be pushed back, but when at all possible, do your best to allot enough time to use as few translators as possible.

5. Linguists specialize in language, not business

The translation industry is dominated by hundreds of small agencies owned and operated by linguists. While these people may do an excellent job of managing translation projects, their expertise may not include business savvy and customer-service skills. Be sure that you are confident in the business practices and professionalism of the agency you select, with it is small or large. A little extra time spent screening agencies upfront will save you many hours in the long run.

6. Everyone will guarantee high-quality translation

How do you measure translation quality? This question is about as easy to answer as how one would measure the quality of a novel or a poem. Writing is subjective, so it stands to reason that translation is as well. Of course, calculating every typo or mistranslation found is one way to measure quality, but it should not be the only way.

The best way to ensure high-quality output is to begin at the source, which means the source text. You will get better results if your source text is translation-ready—shorter, simpler sentences that are free of cultural references. Then look at the process itself. Did you have a realistic amount of time to complete the project? How many projects are your translators juggling at the same time? Finally, do an evaluation upon the project's completion to ensure your standards for quality were met.

7. Translation agencies do not love machine translation

Five years ago, most translation agencies only pointed to machine translation software when they wished to point out what poor quality it generated. Most people who run translation agencies are linguists, not software developers. So they couldn't see the impact that MT would have on the industry today. And I'm not mentioning this to say that clients should use

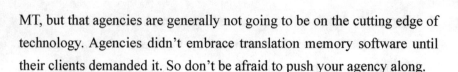

MT, but that agencies are generally not going to be on the cutting edge of technology. Agencies didn't embrace translation memory software until their clients demanded it. So don't be afraid to push your agency along.

Those feelings haven't disappeared. But agencies know that clients are keen on integrating MT into the workflow when feasible, so they have reluctantly embraced MT tools. But machine translation has commoditized translation in a way that agencies can't help but view as a threat. Clients see software that translates for free and they naturally want to apply that tool to every piece of content.

8. Certification doesn't necessarily translate into higher quality

The International Organization for Standardization (ISO.org) has over the years developed a wide range of industry specific standards, such as ISO 9000—a family of quality management standards. Many translations agencies have invested a great deal of time and money to become certified under a number of these standards, and they go to great lengths to advertise this. In fact, some clients limit their agency selection process to considering only those agencies that have specific certifications. You'll see this most in the regulated industries, such as the medical and government sectors.

But certification itself does not guarantee quality. Certification is about process, which is important but is not perfect. People are still the ones managing your translation, and people can still make mistakes, cut corners, or otherwise put projects at risk. Be sure that certification is only one of many areas you examine when selecting an agency.

9. Two different agencies may use the same translators

Because so many agencies outsource so much work, it's not unlikely that you could be using many of the same individual translators even if you have more than one agency. This is why it's valuable to know the individual translators who are working on your project. Agencies should be fully transparent about their contractors.

10. Translation agencies are often underutilized

Finally, be sure to make the best use of your translation agency. That is, take full advantage of their cultural and market expertise. Many agency executives have decades of experience watching companies succeed (and fail) around the world. This knowledge is quite valuable.

A number of agencies are beginning to charge for "cultural" and "market entry" consulting, but others will give you this type of advice for free. If so, make the most of it. Ask what your translators think of your product or service or software *before* they begin to work on it. If they find something confusing or silly, odds are your target audience will too. Encourage your agency to act like a partner and invite its members to give critical feedback.

Ten Questions to Ask Your Prospective Translation Agency

When selecting a translation agency, plan on asking a lot of questions. You will be placing a great deal of faith in your vendor—faith that your text is being accurately translated and proofread, which, in essence, is faith that you are making a good impression in new markets. In fact, it's best to begin looking at your agency as your business partner, as you will be joined at the hip as you venture into new languages and markets.

The following questions will help you ensure that the agency you select will be the best fit for your needs.

1. How many employees do you have? And for how long?

Try to match the size of your account with the size of your agency. Large agencies may not provide the attention that you require, while smaller agencies may place a higher value on your account. On the other hand, you may find that small agencies can't provide the resources you require. Also be sure to ask what percentage of work is completed by in-house translators vs. freelance translators (see question #7). While there is no right or wrong answer, these types of questions will give you important insight into how your agency operates.

One industry danger is employee churn and burnout, especially for project managers. By asking for the average tenure of employees and by meeting or speaking with a few, you'll quickly get a feel for the environment. Do these people seem happy to be there? Do they enjoy their work? Or do they seem frazzled or distracted? These intangibles don't come across on an RFP, but they can you tell you volumes about an agency.

2. What's your industry specialty?

"We translate anything and everything!" is not the best answer to this question. Try to find an agency that has expertise in your particular industry. Some agencies in this directory spend the bulk of their energies in particular fields, such as automotive, medical, or software. This degree of specialization can be highly valuable because the agency will have a dedicated team of translators and editors familiar with the unique terminology of your industry. And, just to be safe, quiz your prospective project manager on some of your industry terminology. After years of working in specific industries, project managers may know as much about your industry as you do.

3. What's your project specialty?

Different projects often require different agencies. For example, many translation agencies don't have the software engineering expertise to manage software localization projects. And an agency that specializes in print translation and interpretation may offer little help with a web globalization project. Always ask to see samples of the agency's work to make sure the agency will know how to effectively manage your project.

Language specialty also applies here. Not every client wants an agency that handles all languages. Some agencies are selected because they're strong with just a few languages or cultures, such as Spanish for the US market or Eastern European languages.

4. How do you measure and control quality?

No agency is perfect, but the best agencies are the ones that keep track of their mistakes to ensure that they aren't repeated. Some agencies have instituted rigorous quality management processes. Ask for details on how errors are caught, tracked, and reported back to the client.

5. What software do you support?

Make sure that your agency has the correct software tools to support the files you provide. If you rely on highly specialized software, you may be limited by the number of agencies that can support it. Ask for a detailed list of software applications and operating systems. At a minimum, you'll want an agency that supports translation memory and terminology management software. But also look at cloud-based solutions as well as the integration of machine translation.

6. Can I speak with your references?

Always, always check references. Ideally, you should speak with three to five references, and at least one client within your industry. Ask this client about quality of service, costs, and lessons learned.

7. What percentage of your translation is outsourced?

Most multi-language agencies outsource some, if not all, of the actual translation work. This practice is quite common, particularly with smaller agencies, and doesn't necessarily mean that quality will suffer. In fact, some of the most highly qualified translators are independent contractors who work exclusively with a number of agencies. Nevertheless, it is important to know exactly who is translating your text so you can play a role in selecting qualified translators and keeping an eye on quality and consistency. Also find out if the agency outsources project management.

Get a breakdown of what languages are managed in-house vs. outsourced. Next, ask for information on the freelancers you might be using. Can the agency guarantee that you'll get the same freelancers (improving overall consistency)? It's worthwhile to speak with at least one in-house and one freelance translator.

8. Can you conduct a sample translation for us?

The "translator test" is a common practice in this industry, and most, if not all, agencies will gladly conduct a free test translation for you. Provide a sample of the actual project, and pay attention to the process as a whole. Quality is important, but keep in mind that agencies will often devote extra translators to the test. Equally important is to focus on the process—how attentive and helpful were they? Did they ask you the right questions before taking on the test?

As you'll see in our Q&A with Kathleen Bostick of Lionbridge, not everyone is a fan of the sample translation. I don't view a sample translation as the most important criterion, but it is something to be reviewed nonetheless. The real value of a sample translation is the additional interaction you'll have with your prospective agency, not the translation itself. Of course, if the translation quality is shoddy, you'll want to move on.

9. Who is my dedicated contact?

Make sure you have someone, typically a project manager, you can call at a moment's notice, and be sure to work with this person during the test translation. It is important that your contact have excellent communications skills, be responsive, and pay excellent attention to detail. You should know where this person is located and when you'll be able to reach him/her.

10. How can I save money on this project?

A good agency will always suggest ways to save money on your translation project, such as editing down text or removing complex graphics. This type of advice can be invaluable, but only if you receive it *before* you begin the project. The best agencies are those that will help you avoid extra costs—even if it might mean they make less money. These agencies understand that if they help you succeed, then they too will succeed.

Translation Costs

In the end, the cost of your translation project will hinge on the number of words you want translated and the languages you want them translated into. Not all languages are equally expensive to translate. For example, there are thousands of qualified Spanish translators an agency can rely upon, forcing down prices, while qualified Arabic translators are much harder to come by and more expensive to hire. As shown here, translation costs can run from five cents per word all the way up to 30 cents, depending on whether you hire an in-country freelance translator or hire a multi-language vendor.

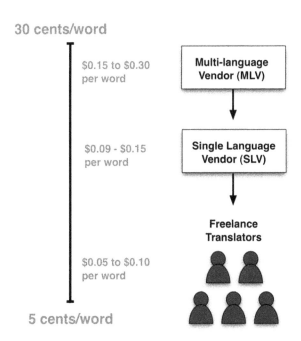

30 cents/word

$0.15 to $0.30 per word — **Multi-language Vendor (MLV)**

$0.09 - $0.15 per word — **Single Language Vendor (SLV)**

Freelance Translators

$0.05 to $0.10 per word

5 cents/word

But keep in mind that there are tradeoffs in quality, risk, and time involved.

An MLV can manage the workflow for you and pass the text through multiple translators, yet if you were to hire your own freelancers, you would have to take on project management duties yourself.

Neither approach is right or wrong; you simply need to be aware of what is involved before you decide which route to take.

The major variables that affect translation costs are:

- **Quantity**: The larger the project, the greater the discount you'll receive.
- **Complexity**: The more technically complex the project is (software vs. Word file) and the more topically complex it is (marketing content vs. medical device instructions) will factor into costs.
- **Timing**: If you need a project returned overnight, expect to pay extra. Agencies will commit to lower prices if you can commit to a more flexible and/or predictable schedule.

So what is a realistic "per word" cost? Below are some sample prices, based on a round of translation, an additional round of editing, and project management. Notice how prices vary by language:

Language pair	Rate (US$)
English > Arabic	0.30
English > Chinese (Simplified)	0.27
English > Chinese (Traditional)	0.27
English > Croatian	0.24
English > Czech	0.24
English > Finnish	0.26
English > French (France)	0.24

English > German	0.24
English > Japanese	0.28
English > Korean	0.28

Also keep in mind that the more complex the subject matter and the project is, the greater the final costs will be. For example, translating a general business letter is going to be less expensive than clinical instructions for a medical device because the pool of qualified translators will be much smaller and generally more expensive to hire.

What should be included in the translation costs

- Use of one or several native, educated, and experienced translators
- Use of a second translator in each language to edit and proofread each file
- Use of an industry specialist as content manager or proofreader
- General formatting in commonly used software programs (Word, Excel)
- Project management and file management
- Account management

What volume can a translator handle?

The general rule of thumb is 2,500 words per day, or 10 pages of a Word document. Editors can handle greater volume, more than 4,000 words per day. And, of course, the use of translation memory tools can greatly increase productivity.

Reading a Translation Quote

One of the great mysteries of the translation industry is how agencies quote projects. There is no standard formula agencies follow, which leaves you, the client, struggling to make "apple to apple" comparisons among them. However, if you keep the following tips in mind, you'll be better prepared to compare not only quotes among vendors but to read between the lines of quotes.

What's the word count?

Not all agencies use the same word-counting software. Different word counts will naturally lead to different quotes. Always conduct your own word-count analysis of your project so you have a means of comparison with the agency.

Also, make sure your translation cost also includes editing and proofreading. Since many clients will choose vendors based purely on their "per word" translation cost, some agencies, in order to appear less expensive, will list translation costs separately from editing and proofreading. While this level of detail can be useful, it's not very practical since you're not likely to hire the agency to translate and not edit.

It is easy to read?

Localization projects can be complex, so it's important that the price quotes be as easy to read as possible. One of the factors you use in selecting an agency should include the user-friendliness of its price quotes.

On the next page is a price quote template for a web localization project from one of the agencies featured in this book: Eriksen Translations (www.eriksen.com). Eriksen has been using this template for a number of years, which is a sign that it resonates well with a wide range of buyers.

Reading between the lines

The nice thing about Eriksen's quote is how each of the localization processes is cleanly organized and easy to digest quickly. Eriksen stresses that clients should carefully review quotes to be sure that all aspects of their projects are included. For instance, in the case of the localization of your corporate web site into another language, Eriksen advises asking the following questions:

- ○ Who will be compiling the foreign language web-ready files? If your LSP (language service provider) isn't doing this, this is another cost to factor in. If you're working with a CMS (content management system), you also need to determine who will be responsible for uploading the translations into this CMS, and what the costs are for this process.
- ○ Will you be reviewing the actual translations? If so, has your LSP stated what costs would be involved in the review and implementation of this feedback?
- ○ Before any web site goes live, each language version needs to be carefully reviewed—is this included in your quotation?

QUOTE

#[sample]

Dear [sample]:

Thank you for contacting Eriksen Translations regarding the **localization of [sample]**. Below please find our quote:

FILE PREPARATION
We provide file preparation at the following rate:

Language	Hours	Rate	Subtotal
Source 1 into Target 1	0	$0.00	$000.00

TRANSLATION
Based on our estimated word count, we provide translation, editing, and proofreading services at the following rate:

Language	Word Count	Rate per Word	Subtotal
Source 1 into Target 1	0,000	$0.00	$000.00

VALIDATION & IMPLEMENTATION OF CLIENT REVIEW CHANGES
We validate and implement your suggested changes at the following rate:

Language	Hours	Rate	Subtotal
Source 1 into Target 1	0	$0.00	$000.00

WEB-BASED GRAPHICS LOCALIZATION
We localize web-based graphics (such as navigational buttons, rollover images, and Flash animations) at the following rate:

Language	Hours	Rate	Subtotal
Source 1 into Target 1	0	$0.00	$000.00

WEBSITE POST-LOCALIZATION TESTING & BUG FIXING
We provide functional testing, in-context linguistic review and bug fixing of the live files posted on your staging site at the following rate:

Language	Hours	Rate	Subtotal
Source 1 into Target 1	0	$0.00	$000.00

PROJECT MANAGEMENT
We will charge a 10% project management fee. This includes set-up, coordination, and ongoing support before and during the project.

TURNAROUND
Your project will require X business days for translation and an additional X business days for validation and implementation of client review changes, graphics localization, and post-localization testing and bug fixing. Rush services are also available at an additional charge.

SUMMARY
The total estimated fee for this project will be $0,000.00. The final fee will be based on the actual files submitted for localization.

Inside the Agency: Q&A with Lionbridge

We interviewed Kathleen Bostick, VP of Global Marketing at Lionbridge (featured in the Agency Profiles section). Kathleen has more than 15 years of experience in the translation industry and manages Lionbridge's multilingual social media and blogging efforts.

You say that sample translations are not the best way to evaluate a translation agency. Explain why.

Most sample translations don't allow language service providers (LSPs) to follow standard translation processes and often forces them to break industry best practices. These best practices are designed to give customers the highest quality translations within the context of a real project. For example:

- A glossary that establishes terminology in the target languages is critical for quality translation. Best practice is to obtain a current glossary or develop one with client input before beginning the actual translation. In most sample translations, no glossary is provided, nor is there time to create one.
- Style guides govern tone, usage of terminology, punctuation, sentence structure, date/time/number formats, etc. With test translation projects, a style guide is rarely, if ever, provided.
- Product training is very important to translators. The companies that receive the highest quality translations from their LSPs invest in training the vendor's resources. Sample translations

rarely ever have associated training.

- Over the course of a normal translation process, translators ask questions about source content to ensure they understand it correctly. During the sample translation process, Q&A is rare and translators are left to guess. This is like being asked to paint a house and guessing what color the customer wants.

- To provide the highest quality translations, LSPs enlist translators who are subject-matter experts in certain areas. These experts are in high demand and are booked well in advance of projects to ensure the right resources are working with the right customers. Sample translations assume the best resources are available "on demand," with the resources being removed from paid projects to address a sample with a quick turnaround, typically for content that is highly specialized and the most difficult to translate in a test setting.

- Clients often request that test translations be completed in two or three days. This simply does not allow for all of the optimal steps to take place (i.e., kickoffs, information exchanges, Q&A). It is nearly impossible to engage the right resources without adequate lead time and when translations are due back immediately.

Here's the approach I recommend for clients who want to test the quality of a language service provider:

- Ask for samples of work from similar customers to assess the supplier's work quality in a particular domain. By providing already-translated materials that comply with the LSP's best practices, customers will be able to more realistically review and evaluate the work quality.

- Ask for in-depth information about the LSP's project

methodologies, quality steps, and overall process.

- o Be clear about your perceived success criteria. Ensure that the LSP understands the resources you believe are required for success on your project and ask for validation that the LSP is able to secure the right resources.
- o If you believe it is critical to assess the LSP's work on a live job, conduct a small paid pilot project. You can control the time and cost of evaluating the materials by short listing LSPs and asking only two to complete the project. The benefit here is that you end up with translations that you will actually use, so your money is not spent redoing already translated material.

To what extent is machine translation taking the place of human translation?

The use of machine translation is not appropriate for all projects and all content types. Machine translation is optimally applied when:

- o The work consists of large projects and/or large word counts.
- o Customers understand that getting both high quality and low price may not be possible without understanding tradeoffs.
- o Quality of the source text to be translated is very high and/or written in a controlled language.
- o The content is technical and/or simple text; marketing content and other type of creative or free-style content are not appropriate.
- o Well-developed glossaries and existing, high-quality translation memories.

If all the above criteria are met, MT may take the place of the initial round of translation, with post-editing by a trained linguist following the MT effort. However, for smaller projects, projects with "complex" content, projects where there is no TM or glossary, or projects where high-quality results are of key importance, machine translation will likely play no role. (Post-editing in the latter may outweigh any benefit gained by MT in the first place.)

What is the main reason for companies using translation memories—money savings, time savings, or increased quality?

I would say all three. Translation memories allow your language service provider to work more quickly, cheaply, and effectively for you. Here are some of the benefits of TM:

- Better consistency and quality because the approved translation is always used, and all subsequent translations will employ the same pre-approved phrasing.
- Faster translation times because the translator can focus on just new material.
- Lower costs because once the TM contains a critical mass of approved translations, a significantly smaller portion of any new document needs to be translated.

To be clear though, setting up a TM does require an upfront investment in time. The TM is typically a dedicated database of source text and the equivalent translations. Over time, as you add translated projects to it, the TM grows in size and scope. Eventually, it greatly enhances the speed and quality of your LSP's work, with consistency and efficiency.

When does it make sense to NOT use translation memory?

It does not make sense use a TM if the original translation was determined to be poor. Even if a TM is in a non-standard format and needs to be converted to an industry standard format, the benefit of using those past translations makes up for the small loss of leverage during conversion.

How do you measure translation quality?

This is the million-dollar question, since language quality can be very subjective. Quality means different things to different buyers. It is easier to describe how you control quality than how you measure it. In brief, how you control quality involves:

- o Quality at source—choosing the right translators that have specific subject-matter expertise. For example, you would not use the same translator to translate games as you would medical devices. They need to be subject-matter experts.
- o QA steps such as editing and proofreading by a second qualified linguist.
- o Any automatic checks that review for punctuation, grammar (according to basic rules), sentence length, untranslated segments, etc.
- o Client review and/or other third-party linguistic review.
- o Usability testing for technical documentation, in which a usability tester can work through the instructions and verify that they get the intended result.

If a company doesn't have an in-country office to do a review, what should they do?

I would recommend looking for an LSP that has an independent linguistic review service. This service consists of independent third-party linguists who perform reviews of the localized text and deliver a bug report listing errors, category of severity, and suggestions for changes. Lionbridge offers this service through the LQS (Language Quality Services) division. LQS independently reviews translations from Lionbridge's customers as well as other LSPs.

What do you recommend if companies wish to take their blogs global?

This is a very real challenge and many companies are experimenting with best practices in this area. Blog writing is very casual, but you can still train your writers on the best practices for writing for localization (which are the same principles, essentially, that are involved in writing for a global audience, a non-native English audience, and/or machine translation).

At Lionbridge, we are currently in the process of taking our blog global. We are adopting a hybrid approach, where some of our content will be created and translated centrally. This content will make up the core of our blog. We will then supplement with locally created content that is relevant to a particular market. The biggest challenge in blogging is maintaining fresh and relevant content that engages readers. We know readers are more likely to engage with blogs when the content is in their native language, so providing content in the local language is a necessity.

The first step for us is to move our blog to a more robust platform, such as a content management system (CMS) that can manage multiple languages. We will then integrate the CMS with Freeway, our translation management system. Freeway allows users to identify content to be translated and route it to translation. We have committed to translating our core, "long shelf life" blog content into 18 languages. One added benefit of producing blog content that is translated and optimized for local key words is increased findability by search engines.

The next step will be to recruit local subject-matter experts to write content in local language on topics relevant to that country. This is a tougher challenge, as not all in-country offices have local subject-matter experts and writers. We have started this process and have a core team in Poland ready to write and share their knowledge.

A third step will be to integrate a customized real-time translation tool with the blog. We will use this approach to address the content and languages that will not be translated by humans due to time or money constraints. If the blog posts are well-written, an automatic translation solution like the customized Lionbridge RTTS solution may be the best bet for achieving "good enough," "just in time" translations that are cost effective. This content does not need award-winning translations, but in-language content will reach our intended audiences more effectively than English-only content.

Lastly, we will have in-country resources available to monitor any comments posted to the blog and respond appropriately in the local language. Taking a blog global is a huge undertaking, but I'm confident it will be worth the effort. I'll know more next year at this time!

Taking the Mobile App Global: Q&A with Glyph Language Services

We interviewed Aaron Schliem, co-founder of Glyph Language Services (featured in the Agency Profiles section) on what companies should know before localizing their mobile applications.

What types of apps have you localized and into what languages?

Glyph has localized a bit of everything, including games, business utilities, travel utilities, recreation apps (geo caching, for example), home economy apps, email clients...and certainly our share of fun train-ride-time-fillers. As for languages, we have worked into French, Spanish, Brazilian Portuguese, Italian, German, Dutch, Russian, Simplified Chinese, Traditional Chinese, Korean, Japanese, Swedish, and Norwegian. For mobile browser-based apps, the list extends to include Arabic, Thai, and Finnish.

What are the most common mistakes companies make when sending apps to be localized?

As with any digital content, companies often do not know where all the content resides. With Android it tends to be easier because they are already thinking XML, but with iPhone, many do not know how to work with the existing SDK tools that Apple provides to export the ".strings" file (and at a deeper level how to use proper syntax in the code so that the SDK tools can do their job).

Another key mistake is that companies forget about the marketing side of their investment. They are not always thinking about getting their iTunes descriptions and keywords localized or creating a mini-site for users to learn more about the app, or maybe discover other apps.

Any tips for companies that haven't yet developed mobile apps—so that they can build apps that are more "world ready" from the beginning?

Think carefully about which markets you want to target and what the current trends are as they relate to device penetration, availability of app stores (including paid apps) in the target languages, and cultural factors that may affect buying habits (i.e., if you have a mileage counter app, don't localize it for a market with very low levels of car usage). From a technical standpoint, think through your content localization cycle and update requirements before you start writing code. Nothing worse that trying to drive 200 kph in a car that was designed for a leisurely Sunday drive.

Since mobile apps generally have very little text, how do you charge for a project?

Glyph has an aggressive strategy for "minimum fee" pricing because many of our clients in the worlds of mobile, games, social media, and even old-school software development are facing increasing pressure to provide agile content/feature releases. Agile tends to lead to small word counts per release (and demanding timelines).

We have an internal workflow that aside from allowing us to keep the agile process afloat, gives us bottom-line cost advantages and, ultimately, pricing flexibility. As with any other pricing negotiation, a key factor is the expected trajectory over time and the degree to the which the client is willing to work with Glyph to create a predictable and structured workflow.

What are the most popular languages for mobile app localization?

Pretty similar to the rest of the industry really—German, French, Spanish, and Japanese as the core. Decent amount of Korean and Brazilian Portuguese. Not as much Russian and Chinese compared to PC applications. My gut perception is that app developers tend to be afraid of Asia in general, opting for Western Europe as a more predictable and mature landscape with regard to mobile payment regimes and smartphone market penetration. Although Japanese is certainly a viable market, many seem to be intimidated by the high demands of advanced Japanese mobile consumers.

Given the personal nature of so many mobile apps, to what extent must they be re-engineered to adapt to specific cultures and countries?

To be honest, in my experience, the time that most developers invest in a mobile app makes it not very attractive to re-engineer apps for unique markets. Either the app is complex and utilitarian and probably doesn't need much adapting, or it is more of a pop culture "hit or miss" initiative. In the latter case, the logic is to ride the wave with what you have as long as you can and in as many markets as you can. By the time you were to re-engineer for a new market, it's possible that the moment will have passed, the wave subsided. I sense that most would prefer to just bust out a brand-new app for the special target market that fits their idiosyncrasies.

What questions should a company ask when selecting a vendor to take its apps global?

What is your strategy for managing encoding transformation during the work cycle and ultimately ensuring proper encoding of deliverables (in particular UTF-16 encoding for iPhone apps)?

How does your company handle .strings file parsing? What is your approach to testing localized apps on live devices?

To what extent can companies save money by localizing apps across multiple platforms (iOS, Android, Windows)?

Saving money across platforms is very much about content repositories and file parsing. A good TM can be applied across all of these core platforms as long as your loc vendor can get at the content in a clean way.

Do you have any data to illustrate how app localization improves overall success?

Clients have indicated to us that localization tends to make their international revenue streams more predictable. They existed prior to localization, but after localization they grew and could be used as a source of business planning data. The folks at Nokia have indicated that app sales tend to increase by 18 to 22 percent when developers make the app available in the local language.

Glyph recently conducted an informal study of iTunes App Store rankings across 11 markets in the Americas, Europe, and Asia to see how many of the top 20 apps were localized and how many apps had localized app store descriptions. As you can see in the graphic below, many companies invest in app localization without also localizing their app store descriptions.

Top 20 iPhone Apps

Market	# Apps localized	# Descr. only localized	Total # Apps w/ some localization
Canada (French)	8	0	8
Mexico (Spanish)	6	1	7
Brazil (Portuguese)	9	2	11
France (French)	12	4	16
Italy (Italian)	15	2	17
Germany (German)	9	5	14
Spain (Spanish)	10	2	12
Japan (Japanese)	16	0	16
Korea (Korean)	16	2	18
China (Simplified Chinese)	12	0	12
Taiwan (Traditional Chinese)	6	0	6

Data from May 2010

Agency Directory

This section includes profiles of 44 translation agencies. The information was provided by the agencies themselves and edited for clarity and space. Agencies did not pay to be included in this guide. The purpose of this section is to help you quickly develop a short list of agencies based on your needs and their qualifications.

Although this section includes many of the world's largest and most respected agencies, it is by no means comprehensive. There are many excellent agencies that were not included. I encourage you to conduct additional research, particularly checking references, before making an agency selection.

Agencies by Size

There are a number of criteria you can use when selecting a translation agency, one being the size of the agency. While there is no rule that says a large agency cannot handle a small translation project (or vice versa) we have found that clients are more likely to have a positive experience when their translations needs are in line with the capabilities of their translation vendors.

In other words, if you have a small translation project, you're better off looking at smaller vendors than vendors that specialize in million-dollar projects. However, if you think that today's small project might quickly grow into tomorrow's large project, it's best to select an agency that can quickly grow to meet your growing needs.

The list below groups agencies by size based on their past or projected revenues. Only two agencies in this list (Lionbridge and SDL) are publicly owned, which means all other agencies have self-reported their revenue range to us.

$50 million+
- Lionbridge (Projected 2010 revenues: $300+ million)
- SDL (2009 revenues: $272 million)
- TransPerfect (Projected 2010 revenues: $250 million)
- Welocalize (Projected 2010 revenues: $60 million)

$20 million to $30 million
- CSOFT International

$10 million to $20 million

- Acclaro
- Argos Translations
- Globalization Partners International
- LUZ
- One Hour Translation ($10 to $50 million)
- Wordbank Limited

$5 million to $10 million

- CPSL (Celer Pawlowsky, SL)
- Eriksen Translations
- E-C Translation
- Jiangsu Sunyu Information Technology Co.
- Lingo24
- LinguaLinx
- Matrix Communications
- Net-Translators
- PTIGlobal

$1 million to $5 million

- American Translation Partners, Inc.
- Ccaps Translation and Localization
- Glyph Language Services
- Hermes Traducciones y Servicios Lingüísticos
- HighTech Passport
- Idea Factory Languages
- International Language Services
- Kwintessential
- Language Connect
- Lingotek
- Lingua Tech Singapore

- MAGNUS
- Schreiber Translations, Inc. (STI)
- Syzygy Information Services
- Translation Plus
- TripleInk

$500,000 to $1 million

- In Every Language
- InterNation
- Multimedia Languages & Marketing
- New Market Translations
- World Language Communications

Less than $500,000

- Accuphrase
- AST Language Services
- TransAction Translators

Agencies by Location

Despite the advantages of email and the Internet, many clients still prefer hiring local agencies. There is a comfort factor in knowing you can physically visit with your agency without hopping on a plane.

Below are the agencies included in this guide, segmented by headquarters location. Please note that about half of these agencies have more than one office around the world, sometimes quite a few. SDL, for example, has 60 offices.

ASIA PACIFIC

Australia
- Multimedia Languages & Marketing

China
- CSOFT International
- E-C Translation
- Jiangsu Sunyu Information Technology Co.

Singapore
- Lingua Tech Singapore

Taiwan
- Syzygy Information Services

Europe

Cyprus
- One Hour Translation

Germany
- Matrix Communications

Poland
- Argos Translations

Spain
- CPSL (Celer Pawlowsky, SL)
- Hermes Traducciones y Servicios Lingüísticos

UK
- AST Language Services
- Kwintessential
- Language Connect
- Lingo24
- SDL
- TransAction Translators
- Wordbank Limited

The Americas

British Virgin Islands
- Idea Factory Languages

Brazil
- Ccaps Translation and Localization

United States
- California
  - HighTech Passport
  - LUZ
  - MAGNUS
  - Net-Translators
  - World Language Communications
- Kentucky
  - In Every Language
- Maryland
  - Schreiber Translations, Inc. (STI)
  - Welocalize
- Massachusetts
  - American Translation Partners
  - Lionbridge Technologies
- Minnesota
  - International Language Services, Inc. (ILS)
  - TripleInk
- New Jersey
  - Accuphrase
  - New Market Translations
  - Translation Plus

- ○ New York
  - Acclaro
  - Eriksen Translations
  - InterNation
  - LinguaLinx Language Solutions
  - TransPerfect Translations International

- ○ Oregon
  - PTIGlobal

- ○ Utah
  - Lingotek

- ○ Washington
  - Glyph Language Services

- ○ Washington, D.C.
  - Globalization Partners International

Agencies by Specialization

Don't underestimate the importance of specialization. If you're a medical device manufacturer, you want translators who understand the difference between a stent and a catheter. Terminology or tactical expertise can often make or break a translation project. Even if you are creating mass-market promotional materials, you want an agency that translates your materials with a tone appropriate to your audience. For many years, there was little in the way of agency specialization. Today, however, agencies have carved out profitable businesses by focusing on one or two industry verticals.

The following is a selective list of agencies segmented by specialty. We asked each agency to select no more than three categories, so please note that many agencies could easily be included across multiple categories, particularly the large and extra-large agencies such as Welocalize, Trans-Perfect, Lionbridge, and SDL.

Automotive
- Argos Translations
- Hermes Traducciones y Servicios Lingüísticos
- Jiangsu Sunyu Information Technology Co.

Chinese for the US
- E-C Translation
- Syzygy Information Services

Consumer Goods/Advertising
- Acclaro

- LinguaLinx Language Solutions
- Translation Plus
- TripleInk

eLearning

- Globalization Partners International
- Lionbridge

Financial & Legal Services

- AST Language Services
- Eriksen Translations
- Kwintessential
- Matrix Communications

Industrial/heavy equipment

- International Language Services, Inc. (ILS)

Legal

- Schreiber Translations
- TransAction Translators
- World Language Communications

Marketing collateral/product documentation

- InterNation
- Lingo24
- Multimedia Languages & Marketing
- One Hour Translation
- PTIGlobal
- Translation Plus

Medical device/pharmaceutical/health care

- Accuphrase
- LUZ
- In Every Language
- Language Connect
- MAGNUS

Software Localization

- CSOFT International
- HighTech Passport
- Net-Translators
- PTIGlobal
- Lionbridge
- SDL

Spanish for the US

- American Translation Partners
- CPSL (Celer Pawlowsky, SL)
- Idea Factory Languages

Telecommunications

- Lingotek
- Lingua Tech Singapore
- New Market Translations

Travel and Entertainment

- Wordbank Limited

Video game localization

- Glyph Language Services

Web globalization

- ○ Lionbridge
- ○ SDL
- ○ TransPerfect Translations
- ○ Welocalize

Agency Profiles

The 44 agencies in this section are sorted alphabetically by company name. We asked the same questions of all agencies; not all questions were answered, and some answers may have been edited for clarity and space. In some cases, companies did not supply client lists due to confidentially provisions.

In all cases, we recommend verifying information by personally contacting client references. Take your time when reviewing agencies. Asks questions. Ideally, you will be selecting an agency that will be your partner for many years to come.

Acclaro

www.acclaro.com

FOUNDED IN:	2002
EMPLOYEES:	60 (400 FREELANCERS)
LANGUAGES:	50+
HEADQUARTERS:	IRVINGTON, NY, USA
ADDITIONAL OFFICES:	BOSTON; SAN FRANCISCO; WASHINGTON, D.C.; BANGKOK; BUENOS AIRES; LONDON
SALES CONTACT:	MICHAEL KRIZ 914-468-0202
	MKRIZ@ACCLARO.COM

Selected Clients
- Amway
- Coach
- LinkedIn
- NetApp
- Sony
- Symantec
- Thomson Reuters

Project Specialization
- PC/Mac software globalization
- Web site globalization
- Product documentation/instructions

Industry Specialization
- Software
- Consumer goods/retail
- Health care

What languages do you expect to add over the next 12 months?

We are seeing more interest in African and Indian languages and expect to expand our teams there.

Which translation software platforms do you support?

SDL Trados, GlobalSight, WorldServer, Passolo, Catalyst, memoQ, ForeignDesk (client-specified commercial tools, custom client interfaces)

What percentage of your translation is currently performed "in the cloud"?

30-40%

Do you support machine translation? If so, what software do you use?

Yes, by client request only. The tool depends on the language pair and client solution required.

What are the hottest industry trends that you are noticing now?

Automating the multilingual content process between the corporate CMS and the suppliers' project and translation workflow system. This should have little, if any, hard cost while significantly reducing the cycle time and effort required to translate content updates and thus keeping all languages in synch with the English source.

Also, trying blended and tiered approaches that mix crowdsourcing and machine translation with professional translation solutions. Both of these have thus far produced more hype than success stories. Neither is easy to deploy successfully. But under the right conditions and for specific types of projects, they might be worth piloting.

Accuphrase

www.accuphrase.com

FOUNDED IN:	2007
EMPLOYEES:	2 (60+ FREELANCERS)
LANGUAGES:	100+
HEADQUARTERS:	HADDONFIELD, NJ, USA
SALES CONTACT:	BJORN KOMMEDAL 856-528-3816
	INFO@ACCUPHRASE.COM

Selected Clients
- Amgen
- GSK
- Morphotek
- Novo Nordisk
- Roche

Project Specialization
- Web site globalization
- Marketing collateral
- Product documentation/instructions

Industry Specialization
- Medical device/pharma
- Health care

What languages do you expect to add over the next 12 months?
Our latest expansion area has been and still is Indian languages.

Which translation software platforms do you support?
SDL Trados

What are the hottest industry trends that you are noticing now?

The trends within pharma translation seem to be pretty conservative, probably trailing behind the more technical areas of localization. The most dominant trend that comes to mind is greater diversification in TM tools.

American Translation Partners

www.americantranslationpartners.com

FOUNDED IN:	1996
EMPLOYEES:	8 (3,500 FREELANCERS)
LANGUAGES:	200+
HEADQUARTERS:	RAYNHAM, MA, USA
ADDITIONAL OFFICE:	REPUBLIC OF PANAMA
SALES CONTACT:	SCOTT CRYSTAL 508-823-8892
	SCOTT@AMERICANTRANSLATIONPARTNERS.COM

Selected Clients
- Honda Research and Development (USA)
- American Tower Corporation
- Staples
- Lahey Clinic
- Boston Children's Hospital
- Kenney Manufacturing
- Boston University

Project Specialization
- Web site globalization
- Marketing collateral
- Product documentation/instructions

Industry Specialization
- Legal
- Health care
- Spanish for US localization

Which translation software platforms do you support?
SDL Trados

Do you support machine translation? If so, what software do you use?

Yes: For Japanese, Atlas V14.

What are the hottest industry trends that you are noticing now?

Certification for medical interpreters; compliancy variances for labor classification of freelance linguists between federal and state laws; outsourcing to India and China as a cheap alternative.

Argos Translations

www.argostranslations.com

FOUNDED IN:	1996
EMPLOYEES:	92 (3,000 FREELANCERS)
LANGUAGES:	60+
HEADQUARTERS:	KRAKÓW, POLAND
ADDITIONAL OFFICES:	CHICAGO, IL, USA; AND GALWAY, IRELAND
SALES CONTACT:	ROBERT FORLOINE 312-714-6260
	INFO@ARGOSTRANSLATIONS.COM

Project Specialization
- PC/Mac software globalization
- Web site globalization
- Product documentation/instructions

Industry Specialization
- Automotive
- Medical device/pharma
- Software

Which translation software platforms do you support?
SDL Trados, XTM Suite, Lionbridge Translation Workspace, Google Translator Toolkit, GlobalSight

Do you support machine translation?
Yes.

Does your firm have any unique capabilities to add?
Argos offers our clients a proprietary suite of translation tools and a translation management system to assist during production, reduce costs, and improve

turnaround.

What sets your agency apart from others?

Strict quality focus (ISO certification—9001:2008, EN15038:2006, LQA and J2450 compliance, EU and OECD approved).

AST Language Services

www.astls.co.uk

FOUNDED IN:	1995
EMPLOYEES:	6 (100+ FREELANCERS)
LANGUAGES:	40+
HEADQUARTERS:	NOTTINGHAM, UK
SALES CONTACT:	MARINA JOHNSON +44 115 9705633
	ENQUIRIES@ASTLS.CO.UK

Selected Clients
o WestLB
o Drambuie
o National Bank of Belgium
o Experian
o Serco
o de Montford University
o PricewaterhouseCoopers

Project Specialization
o Web site globalization
o Marketing collateral
o Product documentation/instructions

Industry Specialization
o Financial
o Legal
o Industrial/heavy equipment

What languages do you expect to add over the next 12 months?
Thai, Indonesian

Which translation software platforms do you support?

SDL Trados, XTM Suite, memoQ, Transit

Does your firm have any unique capabilities to add?

International telemarketing

Ccaps Translation and Localization

www.ccaps.net

FOUNDED IN:	1999
EMPLOYEES:	18 (120+ FREELANCERS)
LANGUAGES:	ENGLISH, BRAZILIAN PORTUGUESE, LATIN AMERICAN SPANISH
HEADQUARTERS:	RIO DE JANEIRO, BRAZIL
SALES CONTACT:	FABIANO CID +55 21 2507 5989
	FCID@CCAPS.NET

Selected Clients
- Oracle
- SAP
- VMware
- McDonald's
- Xerox
- Shell
- Lavazza

Project Specialization
- PC/Mac software globalization
- Product documentation/instructions
- Audio/Video localization/dubbing

Industry Specialization
- Software
- Computers and peripherals
- Telecommunications

What languages do you expect to add over the next 12 months?

European Portuguese and European Spanish

Which translation software platforms do you support?

SDL Trados, memoQ

What percentage of your translation is currently performed "in the cloud"?

10%

Do you support machine translation? If so, what software do you use?

Yes: We use machine translation post editing and MT via Asia Online.

Does your firm have any unique capabilities to add?

Marketing translation: Translation of slogans, taglines, punch lines, etc., and brand assessment performed by senior professionals with diverse backgrounds.

The process includes personal or over-the-phone interviews with clients, who then respond to a questionnaire with their basic requirements. Ccaps then delivers several options with back translation and audio-recorded versions of the suggested translations.

What are the hottest industry trends that you are noticing now?

Outsourced project management and repositioning of Latin America as a viable alternative to Asia.

What sets your agency apart from others?

Expertise in the Latin American market.

CPSL (Celer Pawlowsky, SL)

www.cpsl.com

FOUNDED IN:	1963
EMPLOYEES:	41 (3,400 FREELANCERS)
LANGUAGES:	ALL LANGUAGES, WITH SPECIALIZATION IN SPANISH.
HEADQUARTERS:	BARCELONA, SPAIN
ADDITIONAL OFFICES:	MADRID, SPAIN; GERMANY; US; UK
SALES CONTACT:	MARIA KANIA-TASAK
	MKANIA@CPSL.COM

Selected Clients
- Alstom
- Oracle
- European Parliament
- The Global Fund
- AVG
- D-Link
- Garmin

Project Specialization
- PC/Mac software globalization
- Web site globalization
- Product documentation/instructions

Industry Specialization
- Medical device/pharma
- Industrial/heavy equipment
- Spanish for US localization

Which translation software platforms do you support?
STAR Transit, Across, WorldServer

Do you support machine translation? If so, what software do you use?

Yes: T-Text.

What are the hottest industry trends that you are noticing now?

Companies require a supplier that is able to manage the entire lifecycle of documents from creating, editing, and localizing to multimedia printing.

What sets your agency apart from others?

We organize multilingual events and manage an extensive database of interpreters who work in a wide range of language combinations and are highly specialized.

CSOFT International

www.csoftintl.com

FOUNDED IN:	2003
EMPLOYEES:	430 (5,000+ FREELANCERS)
LANGUAGES:	96
HEADQUARTERS:	BEIJING, CHINA
ADDITIONAL OFFICES:	NEW YORK CITY; SHREWSBURY, MA; FORT LAUDERDALE; SUNNYVALE, CA; HOPKINS, MN; GOTHENBURG, SWEDEN; DÜSSELDORF, GERMANY; SHANGHAI, CHINA; OSAKA, JAPAN; PRESTON, AUSTRALIA
SALES CONTACT:	MATT ARNEY 415-868-5106
	MATT.ARNEY@CSOFTINTL.COM

Selected Clients
- P&G
- Dell
- Yahoo
- Adobe
- Intel
- Medtronic
- AMD

Project Specialization
- PC/Mac software globalization
- Web site globalization
- Product documentation/instructions

Industry Specialization
- Medical device/pharma
- Software

- Computers and peripherals

Which translation software platforms do you support?
SDL Trados, Wordbee Translator, Google Translator Toolkit, GlobalSight

What % of your translation is currently performed "in the cloud"?
Around 5%.

Do you support machine translation? If so, what software?
Normally, we don't use machine translation for translation projects. However, if clients request machine translation services, we can provide these. The applications we use include Client for Google Translate, Transtar, Moses, ProMT Translator, etc.

Does your firm have any unique capabilities to add?
Many of our founding members were actively involved in the development of first-generation language and translation technology before localization was a recognized industry, and we have one of the largest technical infrastructures and resource centers on the continent. This technical focus has enabled us to develop innovative, practical, and highly collaborative tools, like the world's first wiki-based terminology management tool, TermWiki, and the first browser-based visual translation review tool, ReviewIT.

What are the hottest industry trends that you are noticing now?
A move toward cloud-based review and terminology management, collaborative authoring and translation, and post-MT editing.

What sets your agency apart from others?
CSOFT is one of the few LSPs to gain both ISO 9001:2008 and 13485-2003 certifications. In recognition of this devotion to quality, Kodak, Carestream Health, and Dell have all presented CSOFT with quality vendor awards.

E-C Translation

www.e-cchina.com

FOUNDED IN:	1997
EMPLOYEES:	201 (1,000+ FREELANCERS)
LANGUAGES:	52 LANGUAGES, WITH SPECIALIZATION IN CHINESE, GERMAN, FRENCH, SPANISH, ITALIAN, RUSSIAN, JAPANESE, KOREAN, AND THAI
HEADQUARTERS:	BEIJING, CHINA
ADDITIONAL OFFICES:	SHENYANG, CHENGDU, SHANGHAI, AND HONG KONG; SINGAPORE; IRELAND; IRVINE, CA; PHILADELPHIA; CHICAGO; BELFORD, NJ
SALES CONTACT:	JAMES WE +86 10 67868761 JAMES_WEI@E-CCHINA.COM

Selected Clients
- Siemens
- SAP
- Sybase
- HP
- ESRI
- PTC
- Rockwell

Project Specialization
- PC/Mac software globalization
- Mobile app globalization
- Web site globalization

Industry Specialization
- Medical device/pharma

○ Software
○ Chinese for US localization

Which translation software platforms do you support?
SDL Trados

Does your firm have any unique capabilities to add?
We have developed our own portal for project management, where freelance partners can accept jobs and handle financial issues, and clients can assign projects and monitor progress.

What are the hottest industry trends that you are noticing now?
Machine translation, shared translation memories, and translation/content management systems are all hot topics in the industry.

What sets your agency apart from others?
We were rated "Outstanding Supplier" by Siemens in 2008 and 2009, and a "Top 10 Translation Enterprise" in 2009 and 2010 by Translators Association of China (TAC), the only national association in the field of translation in China.

Eriksen Translations

www.eriksen.com

FOUNDED IN:	1986
EMPLOYEES:	35 (800 FREELANCERS)
LANGUAGES:	100+
HEADQUARTERS:	BROOKLYN, NY, USA
ADDITIONAL OFFICES:	CÓRDOBA, ARGENTINA; SAN DIEGO, CA
SALES CONTACT:	MATT HEENAN 718-802-9010
	MATT.HEENAN@ERIKSEN.COM

Selected Clients
- Skype
- JPMorgan Chase
- NYC Department of Health & Mental Hygiene
- Accenture
- Prudential
- NYU School of Medicine

Project Specialization
- Web site globalization
- Marketing collateral
- Product documentation/instructions

Industry Specialization
- Medical device/pharma
- Software
- Financial

Which translation software platforms do you support?
SDL Trados, Lionbridge Translation Workspace, Transit NXT (Version 4), Déjà Vu X (7.5), Wordfast Pro

What percentage of your translation is currently performed "in the cloud"?
Approximately 20%

Does your firm have any unique capabilities to add?
Eriksen has specialized in the Scandinavian languages since our beginning. In addition, through the work we do with advertising and marketing firms, as well as local government agencies, we have gained significant experience with the nuances of cultural adaptation for the multilingual populations in different locations.

We recently signed a joint venture agreement that gives us a far greater global footprint and more capacity; we can now serve clients locally on five continents.

What are the hottest industry trends that you are noticing now?
New production modes (crowdsourcing, wider TMS adoption, translating in the cloud) and mobile app localization.

Globalization Partners International

www.globalizationpartners.com

FOUNDED IN:	2001
EMPLOYEES:	61 (1,200 FREELANCERS)
LANGUAGES:	52
HEADQUARTERS:	WASHINGTON, D.C., USA
ADDITIONAL OFFICES:	MCLEAN, VA; ROSARIO, ARGENTINA; DUBAI, UAE
SALES CONTACT:	MARTIN SPETHMAN 866-272-5874
	MSPETHMAN@GLOBALIZATIONPARTNERS.COM

Selected Clients
- Abbott
- Burson-Marsteller
- Disney
- iRobot
- McDonald's
- The Venetian
- United Nations

Project Specialization
- Web site globalization
- Marketing collateral
- Audio/Video localization/dubbing

Industry Specialization
- Medical device/pharma
- Consumer goods/retail
- eLearning materials

Which translation software platforms do you support?

SDL Trados, Google Translator Toolkit

What percentage of your translation is currently performed "in the cloud"?

Actual translation, 30%; business processes, 100%

Do you support machine translation? If so, what software do you use?

MT use is client-driven. We have used Language Weaver, Google, and Systran.

Does your firm have any unique capabilities to add?

Multilingual W3D (design, development, deployment); web content management system implementations; and country-specific search engine marketing (SEM-SEO-SEA) including social media localization.

What are the hottest industry trends that you are noticing now?

The need for country-specific search engine marketing services, as well as the need for web content management system implementations.

What advice would you give a company that is looking for a new translation vendor?

Meet the immediate team that will be active on your account.

Glyph Language Services

www.glyphservices.com

FOUNDED IN:	2001
EMPLOYEES:	13 (1,000 FREELANCERS)
LANGUAGES:	100+
HEADQUARTERS:	SPOKANE, WA, USA
ADDITIONAL OFFICE:	MADISON, WI
SALES CONTACT:	DAVE HUNT 206-973-8116
	DAVE@GLYPHSERVICES.COM

Selected Clients
- Microsoft
- Playdom
- Appigo
- Game Show Network
- Swype
- Starbucks
- Amazon

Project Specialization
- Mobile app globalization
- Web site globalization
- Games localization (including text, audio, and graphics for console, online, mobile, and especially social)

Industry Specialization
- Software
- Marketing firms/advertising agencies
- Games and media

What languages do you expect to add over the next 12 months?

We've seen emerging interest in the past couple of years for rare African languages (Bemba, Nyanga) and new demand for Valencian, Briton, and other minority European languages.

Which translation software platforms do you support?

SDL Trados, GlobalSight

Do you support machine translation? If so, what software do you use?

We are looking into a Moses cloud-based implementation to support ongoing work in Spanish and Urdu.

Does your firm have any unique capabilities to add?

Glyph is one of the only localization companies pushing the frontiers of localization in new media and for new platforms. We specialize in games localization, especially for social platforms like Facebook and online games, and in localization of apps, games, and web content for the full range of mobile platforms and devices. We provide linguistic consulting to drive content monitoring technology and mobile text input systems.

What are the hottest industry trends that you are noticing now?

Cloud-based workflows, machine translation and post-editing, and the emergence of small-unit translations (social media content).

Hermes Traducciones y Servicios Lingüísticos

www.hermestrans.com

FOUNDED IN:	1991
EMPLOYEES:	31 (100 FREELANCERS)
LANGUAGES:	ENGLISH, SPANISH (INCLUDING LATIN AMERICAN SPANISH), FRENCH, GERMAN, ITALIAN, PORTUGUESE (BRAZIL AND PORTUGAL), CATALAN, GALIZIAN, BASQUE + OTHERS
HEADQUARTERS:	MADRID, SPAIN
ADDITIONAL OFFICE:	MÁLAGA, SPAIN
SALES CONTACT:	JUAN JOSÉ AREVALILLO +34916407640
	JUANJO.AREVALILLO@HERMESTRANS.COM

Project Specialization
- PC/Mac software globalization
- Web site globalization
- Product documentation/instructions

Industry Specialization
- Automotive
- Medical device/pharma
- Software

Which translation software platforms do you support?
SDL Trados, Lionbridge Translation Workspace, Across, Déjà-Vu, STAR Transit

What percentage of your translation is currently performed "in the cloud"?
20%

Does your firm have any unique capabilities to add?

We offer a proprietary productivity and quality management system.

What are the hottest industry trends that you are noticing now?

Shared translation memories and post-edited machine translations.

What sets your agency apart from others?

Eighty percent of our production is done with in-house employees; we have double quality certification by ISO 9001 and European EN 15038 standards and are the only Spanish company to have a linguistic quality certification by Fundéu/Agencia EFE (the company that regulates and recommends correct Spanish language usage for media worldwide).

HighTech Passport

www.htpassport.com

FOUNDED IN:	1992
EMPLOYEES:	15 (1,500 FREELANCERS)
LANGUAGES:	70 LANGUAGES, WITH SPECIALIZATION IN BIDI LANGUAGES AND LANGUAGES OF DEVELOPING COUNTRIES
HEADQUARTERS:	SAN JOSE, CA, USA
ADDITIONAL OFFICE:	BUCHAREST, ROMANIA
SALES CONTACT:	ANNE-MARIE AUBRESPY　408-453-6303, EXT 14 ANNEMARIE@HTPASSPORT.COM

Selected Clients
- Yahoo!
- PayPal
- Varian Medical Systems
- Marin Software
- Smith Micro
- Coremetrics by IBM
- World Bank

Project Specialization
- PC/Mac software globalization
- Mobile app globalization
- Web site globalization

Industry Specialization
- Medical device/pharma
- Software
- Telecommunications

Which translation software platforms do you support?
SDL Trados, WorldServer SDLX, Catalyst, STAR Transit

Do you support machine translation? If so, what software do you use?
Not yet, due to the high quality requested by our clients, but we are researching it.

Does your firm have any unique capabilities to add?
Localization engineering services, bidi engineering and linguistic expertise; linguistic and functional testing; localization process improvement consulting; enhanced project management for accelerated web-loc, enhanced capabilities for localization into developing country languages (Azerbaijani, all Indic languages, Mongolian, Urdu, etc.).

Idea Factory Languages

www.iflang.com

FOUNDED IN:	2003
EMPLOYEES:	78 (150+ FREELANCERS)
LANGUAGES:	ENGLISH, SPANISH, BRAZILIAN PORTUGUESE, GERMAN, FRENCH, ITALIAN ,SWEDISH
HEADQUARTERS:	BRITISH VIRGIN ISLANDS
ADDITIONAL OFFICES:	ARGENTINA AND BRAZIL
SALES CONTACT:	TEDDY BENGTSSON +54 11 4343 4143
	TEDDY.BENGTSSON@IDEA-FACTORY.NET

Selected Clients
- Symantec
- EMC
- SAP
- Oracle
- Mincom
- AMD
- Halogen

Project Specialization
- PC/Mac software globalization
- Web site globalization
- Product documentation/instructions

Industry Specialization
- Software
- Financial
- Industrial/heavy equipment

Which translation software platforms do you support?

SDL Trados, Google Translator Toolkit, GlobalSight, WorldServer, Wordfast, STAR Transit, Catalyst, Passolo, MultiTerm, plus many proprietary ones.

Do you support machine translation? If so, what software do you use?

Yes: We have worked extensively on MT initiatives together with key clients, cooperating with them to develop solutions and implement post-editing. Most of the work has been done with Systran, but we have experience with several other MT tools/solutions.

Does your firm have any unique capabilities to add?

We have built our own online business and project management tool. Our senior staff is regularly engaged as tutors and instructors at professional training events for the industry.

What are the hottest industry trends that you are noticing now?

Online processing; "International Spanish," i.e., to produce one as opposed to multiple versions of the language; and optimized leveraging when there is a need to produce multiple language versions—for example, to translate into LatAm Spanish (or Portuguese) first, then adapt to European instead of a parallel approach to bring higher cost efficiency.

What sets your agency apart from others?

We are the only independent language services provider with its own production centers in both of the key Latin American language markets. We employ a large number of in-house staff. The majority of our business comes from direct clients, as opposed to multilingual vendors, which is unusual in our region.

In Every Language

www.ineverylanguage.com

FOUNDED IN:	2005
EMPLOYEES:	3 (1,300 FREELANCERS)
LANGUAGES:	60
HEADQUARTERS:	LOUISVILLE, KY, USA
SALES CONTACT:	TERENA BELL 502-213-0317
	TERENABELL@INEVERYLANGUAGE.COM

Selected Clients
- Alzheimer's Association
- Humana
- Shield Environmental
- White Castle
- Whip Mix
- La-Z-Boy
- Martin Luther King, Jr. National Memorial Project Foundation
- Walt Disney

Project Specialization
- Web site globalization
- Marketing collateral
- Product documentation/instructions

Industry Specialization
- Medical device/pharma
- Software

Which translation software platforms do you support?
Wordfast

Does your firm have any unique capabilities to add?

In addition to being WBE (Women Business Enterprise) and DBE (Disadvantage Business Enterprise) certified, we offer expertise and knowledge of languages of limited diffusion, especially African languages.

What are the hottest industry trends that you are noticing now?

Crowdsourcing, an emphasis in training people in languages of limited diffusion, and a greater focus on social responsibility in translation.

What sets your agency apart from others?

Through our Translation Plus Two program, we create economic opportunity for trained translators and interpreters who are economically disadvantaged. For example, when you need Arabic or Somali translation, your translation is performed by women, who are traditionally not allowed to work in these cultures.

What advice would you give a company that is looking for a new translation vendor?

Look for a company that's doing things differently. Concentrate on differences, not the similarities. A company working just like the competition may be less inclined to find new, creative solutions to your needs.

InterNation

www.internationinc.com

FOUNDED IN:	1990
EMPLOYEES:	4 (300 FREELANCERS)
LANGUAGES:	90+
HEADQUARTERS:	NEW YORK CITY, USA
SALES CONTACT:	ERICK DERKATSCH 212-619-5545
	ERICK.DERKATSCH@GMAIL.COM

Selected Clients
- Continental Airlines
- British Airways
- Archer Daniel Midland
- Calvin Klein
- Hoffman La Roche
- Microsoft
- Cisco Systems

Project Specialization
Audio/Video localization/dubbing

Industry Specialization
- Computers and peripherals
- Health care
- Marketing firms/advertising agencies

What languages do you expect to add over the next 12 months?
Zulu, Cebuano, Lithuanian

Which translation software platforms do you support?

SDL Trados, Google Translator Toolkit

What percentage of your translation is currently performed "in the cloud"?

10-15%

Does your firm have any unique capabilities to add?

We maintain our own industrial-strength audio recording facility complemented by an expanding database of guaranteed native voice talent. All video editing, subtitling, and DVD authoring is provided in-house.

What are the hottest industry trends that you are noticing now?

Relentless pressure to lower prices for all services through technology solutions and outsourcing.

What sets your agency apart from others?

InterNation specializes in voice-overs and subtitling for corporate video—we are a niche company. Few agencies can match the multilingual voice talent resources we have accumulated over the years. We actually do our AV work ourselves, in-house, with almost zero outsourcing.

International Language Services (ILS)

www.ilstranslations.com

FOUNDED IN:	1982
EMPLOYEES:	6 (500+ FREELANCERS)
LANGUAGES:	100+
HEADQUARTERS:	MINNETONKA, MN, USA
SALES CONTACT:	BARB SICHEL 952-934-5678
	BSICHEL@ILSTRANSLATIONS.COM

Selected Clients
- St. Jude
- Vermeer
- Ecolab
- Toro
- Medtronic
- BASF

Project Specialization
- Web site globalization
- Marketing collateral
- Product documentation/instructions

Industry Specialization
- Medical device/pharma
- Industrial/heavy equipment
- Market research

Which translation software platforms do you support?

SDL Trados

What sets your agency apart from others?

We have a stable project management team; clients work with the same dedicated project manager over extended periods of time.

Jiangsu Sunyu Information Technology Co.

www.sunyu.com

FOUNDED IN:	1996
EMPLOYEES:	324 (543 FREELANCERS)
LANGUAGES:	ENGLISH, SIMPLIFIED/TRADITIONAL CHINESE, GERMAN, JAPANESE, KOREAN
HEADQUARTERS:	NANJING, CHINA
ADDITIONAL OFFICES:	BEIJING AND SHANGHAI IN CHINA; WASHINGTON, D.C., TOKYO, JAPAN
SALES CONTACT:	MS. LIANGLIANG ZHAO +86 25 8669 1999
	SOPHIAZHAO@SUNYU.COM

Project Specialization
- Mobile app globalization
- Web site globalization
- Product documentation/instructions

Industry Specialization
- Automotive
- Medical device/pharma
- Software

What languages do you expect to add over the next 12 months?
French, Spanish, Russian, Arabic

Which translation software platforms do you support?
SDL Trados, Google Translator Toolkit, GlobalSight

What sets your agency apart from others?

We rely mostly on in-house translators and have strict confidentiality policies, which assures the information security of our clients. We were the first translation company in China to acquire the ISO 27001 certificate.

Kwintessential

www.kwintessential.co.uk

FOUNDED IN:	2004
EMPLOYEES:	16 (1,000+ FREELANCERS)
LANGUAGES:	MORE THAN 40 LANGUAGES, WITH SPECIALIZATION IN EUROPEAN, MIDDLE EASTERN, AND ASIAN LANGUAGES.
HEADQUARTERS:	SOMERSET, UK
ADDITIONAL OFFICES:	US, ARGENTINA, SOUTH AFRICA, AND UAE
SALES CONTACT:	SARAH GRANGE +44 1460 279 900
	SGRANGE@KWINTESSENTIAL.CO.UK

Selected Clients
o BP
o BHP Billiton
o Chanel
o Norton Rose
o Thales
o BBC
o Swarovski

Project Specialization
o Web site globalization
o Marketing collateral
o Product documentation/instructions

Industry Specialization
o Financial
o Legal
o Marketing firms/advertising agencies

Which translation software platforms do you support?
SDL Trados

What percentage of your translation is currently performed "in the cloud"?
20%

Do you support machine translation? If so, what software do you use?
Yes: SDL Trados.

Does your firm have any unique capabilities to add?
We have set ourselves up to offer tailored solutions to certain sectors. For example, because TV/film has specific translation and interpreting needs, we offer services such as fixers, standardized "release forms," subtitling, and post-production language controls.

What are the hottest industry trends that you are noticing now?
A move toward more creative translations rather than transactional translations; increasing demand for Arabic, Chinese, Russian, and Turkish; collaboration among agencies to provide more services to customers; and the use of translation agencies for more than just language translation, i.e., design, localization, cultural consultation, etc.

Language Connect

www.languageconnect.net

FOUNDED IN:	2003
EMPLOYEES:	20 (200 FREELANCERS)
LANGUAGES:	145
HEADQUARTERS:	LONDON, UK
ADDITIONAL OFFICES:	MUNICH, GERMANY; AND MELBOURNE, AUSTRALIA
SALES CONTACT:	TESS HICKISH +44 207 940 8108
	TESS@LANGUAGECONNECT.NET

Selected Clients
- ExxonMobil
- Scottish Parliament
- National Health Service (NHS)
- TNS
- Mövenpick Hotels & Resorts Management AG
- Hilton

Project Specialization
- Web site globalization
- Marketing collateral
- Specialist solutions for the market research industry

Industry Specialization
- Legal
- Health care
- Marketing firms/advertising agencies

Which translation software platforms do you support?
SDL Trados, Google Translator Toolkit, Wordfast

What percentage of your translation is currently performed "in the cloud"?

10%

Do you support machine translation? If so, what software do you use?

Yes: Language Weaver

Does your firm have any unique capabilities to add?

Unique services and technology solutions tailored to specific industries, e.g., verbatim coding service for the market research industry, a collaborative artwork transcreation platform, a proprietary interpreter management system for healthcare, etc.

What are the hottest industry trends that you are noticing now?

Enterprise integration and mergers and acquisitions within the MT technology space.

Lingo24

www.Lingo24.com

FOUNDED IN:	2001
EMPLOYEES:	140 (3,050 FREELANCERS)
LANGUAGES:	100+
HEADQUARTERS:	ABERDEEN, UK
ADDITIONAL OFFICES:	EDINBURGH AND LONDON, UK; TIMISOARA, ROMANIA; PANAMÁ CITY, REPUBLIC OF PANAMA
SALES CONTACT:	ELAINE OLSHANETSKY 631-576-8235 MARKETING@LINGO24.COM

Selected Clients
- Bloomberg
- BBC
- Orange
- MTV
- Royal Bank of Scotland
- BP
- T-Mobile

Project Specialization
- Web site globalization
- Marketing collateral
- Product documentation/instructions

Industry Specialization
- Medical device/pharma
- Financial
- Marketing firms/advertising agencies

Which translation software platforms do you support?

SDL Trados, XTM Suite, Google Translator Toolkit, SDLX, and SDL Passolo

What % of your translation is currently performed "in the cloud"?

All of Lingo24's translation work takes place "in the cloud." Our "Heart" technology includes the translation memory tool XTM, a browser-based interface that allows multiple translators and proofreaders to collaborate in real time, significantly reducing turnarounds. Furthermore, it means that documents for translation and translation memories are accessible online via a browser.

Do you support machine translation? If so, what software do you use?

Post-edited machine translation (PEMT) is an important service level that Lingo24 offers as part of a hybrid translation solution, where it is appropriate for the project's requirements. Our translation memory tool XTM—an integral part of our Heart technology—is integrated with statistical machine translation tool Google Translate, which delivers a high level of pre-editing terminology matching.

Does your firm have any unique capabilities to add?

Our hubs across three continents allow us to operate 24/7—this assures that clients can speak to a Lingo24 team member at any time.

What are the hottest industry trends that you are noticing now?

Right now, a move in the business mindset away from translations being reactive—only having content translated when necessary—to being proactive, with businesses seeking customers in new markets by having their marketing collateral translated. This is a great sign, as it shows many businesses are starting to think of their multilingual customer base as a business opportunity, rather than an afterthought. The other important trend is the move toward establishing standards for translation technology, with the creation of tools where translation and proofreading can take place in the "cloud" in real time, and where knowledge can be shared and used across a range of proprietary software.

Lingotek

www.lingotek.com

FOUNDED IN:	2006
EMPLOYEES:	19 (500 FREELANCERS)
LANGUAGES:	ALL
HEADQUARTERS:	SALT LAKE CITY, UT, USA
SALES CONTACT:	ROB VANDENBERG 801-662-0050
	ROB@LINGOTEK.COM

Selected Clients
- Library of Congress
- CIA
- Adobe
- eBay
- The Church of Jesus Christ of Latter Day Saints
- Intermountain Healthcare
- ZAGG

Project Specialization
- Web site globalization
- Marketing collateral
- Product documentation/instructions

Industry Specialization
- Telecommunications
- Consumer goods/retail
- Health care

Which translation software platforms do you support?
Lingotek's Collaborative Translation Platform

Do you support machine translation? If so, what software do you use?

Yes: Google, Microsoft

Does your firm have any unique capabilities to add?

We offer our own Collaborative Translation Platform which allows for real-time status updates, translation done on the cloud, and cost efficiency.

What are the hottest industry trends that you are noticing now?

Translation done in the cloud, post-editing of MT.

Lingua Tech Singapore

www.linguasg.com

FOUNDED IN:	1996
EMPLOYEES:	25 (300 FREELANCERS)
LANGUAGES:	ASIAN LANGUAGES, ARABIC, FARSI, HEBREW MAJOR EUROPEAN LANGUAGES (FIGSP), MAJOR EASTERN EUROPEAN LANGUAGES, MAJOR LATAM LANGUAGES
HEADQUARTERS:	SINGAPORE
SALES CONTACT:	MR. NICKSON CHENG +65 6324 1181 NICKSON_CHENG@LINGUASG.COM

Selected Clients
- Wyeth
- Reader's Digest
- Siemens AG
- Motorola
- Int'l Customer Loyalty Programmes
- eBay International
- Binatone Electronics International

Project Specialization
- PC/Mac software globalization
- Mobile app globalization
- Web site globalization

Industry Specialization
- Medical device/pharma
- Telecommunications
- Financial

Which translation software platforms do you support?

SDL Trados, memoQ, Wordfast, WorldServer, STAR Transit, Lingobit

Does your firm have any unique capabilities to add?

Technical writing for consumer electronic products; adaptation of publications for specific target market; and multilingual DTP.

What are the hottest industry trends that you are noticing now?

Machine translation, online translation, and crowdsourcing.

What sets your agency apart from others?

Compared to other industries, the localization and translation industry is a relatively new one in Singapore and the Southeast Asia region. We have been focused on localization and translation since its inception and are the only company in this region to have formed an alliance with five other localization and translation companies from around the globe.

LinguaLinx Language Solutions

www.lingualinx.com

FOUNDED IN:	2002
EMPLOYEES:	43 (1,000+ FREELANCERS)
LANGUAGES:	100+
HEADQUARTERS:	COHOES, NY, USA
ADDITIONAL OFFICES:	AUSTIN, TX; BALTIMORE, MD; DES MOINES, IA; NEW YORK CITY; OLYMPIA, WA; PORTLAND, OR; PRINCETON, NJ; SACRAMENTO AND SAN FRANCISCO, CA; BEIJING, CHINA; LONDON, UK
SALES CONTACT:	JAY NISH +1 518 388 9000, EXT.1046
	JNISH@LINGUALINX.COM

Project Specialization
- Web site globalization
- Marketing collateral
- Product documentation/instructions

Industry Specialization
- Consumer goods/retail
- Health care
- Marketing firms/advertising agencies

Which translation software platforms do you support?
SDL Trados, Google Translator Toolkit, GlobalSight, WorldServer, memoQ (authorized reseller), Catalyst, XMetaL (authorized reseller)

What percentage of your translation is currently performed "in the cloud"?
Less than 5%

Do you support machine translation? If so, what software do you use?

We support machine translation in instances where its use is appropriate, and with a client's understanding of its nature, the possible shortcomings of its use, and written consent for its deployment. Systran and a variety of open-source solutions are currently utilized as MT solutions.

Does your firm have any unique capabilities to add?

We provide a full array of content authoring solutions, including translation readiness assessment, RFP consulting, eLearning and curriculum development, content management integration, workflow automation, and multi-channel publishing through GlobalScript—our outsourced documentation division.

What are the hottest industry trends that you are noticing now?

An increasing number of companies in the private sector as well as government agencies are requesting translation, on-site interpretation, and telephonic interpretation services under contract from a single source vendor or as few vendors as possible. There is also an increase in requests for service for the hearing impaired.

Lionbridge Technologies

www.lionbridge.com

FOUNDED IN:	1996
EMPLOYEES:	4,200 (2,000 FREELANCERS)
LANGUAGES:	150+
HEADQUARTERS:	WALTHAM, MA, USA
ADDITIONAL OFFICES:	50 OFFICES IN 25 COUNTRIES
SALES CONTACT:	KATHLEEN BOSTICK 972-207-0888
	KATHLEEN.BOSTICK@LIONBRIDGE.COM

Selected Clients
- Expedia
- Royal Caribbean
- Porsche
- Philips
- Genzyme
- Nokia
- Dell

Project Specialization
- PC/Mac software globalization
- Web site globalization
- Product documentation/instructions

Industry Specialization
- Software and Computers
- Telecommunications
- Life Sciences

What languages do you expect to add over the next 12 months?

We have seen growth in sub-Saharan African languages as well as Indic

159

languages, especially in mobile phones. We will continue to add these long-tail languages as demand dictates.

Which translation software platforms do you support?

SDL Trados, Lionbridge Translation Workspace, Google Translator Toolkit, GlobalSight

Our first choice is Translation Workspace; however, we will use whatever tools our clients require.

What percentage of your translation is currently performed "in the cloud"?

70-80%

Do you support machine translation?

Yes: We use multiple machine translation systems, including IBM RTTS, Systran, Google Translate, Microsoft's MT, and Lionbridge's own MT system.

Does your firm have any unique capabilities to add?

Lionbridge provides content development services, including rich media and elearning; interpretations, including in-person and over-the-phone; multilingual keyword optimization and global search relevance; and product engineering services, including application development, testing, and maintenance.

What sets your agency apart from others?

Our "Freeway platform" brings the critical elements of a global enterprise translation program into a single on-demand, free application available to Lionbridge clients and translation partners.

Freeway enables instant use across the enterprise, immediate addition of new users, and simultaneous release of new features without costly or time-consuming deployments and upgrades. By utilizing the Internet for application delivery, organizations do not have to deploy costly desktop and server technology or maintain disparate systems across groups and divisions.

LUZ

www.luz.com

FOUNDED IN:	1994
EMPLOYEES:	40 (1,200 FREELANCERS)
LANGUAGES:	45+
HEADQUARTERS:	SAN FRANCISCO, CA
ADDITIONAL OFFICES:	LAFAYETTE, CO; LAUSANNE, SWITZERLAND; BUENOS AIRES, ARGENTINA
SALES CONTACT:	MONIQUE RIVAS 415-981-5890, EXT. 115
	MONIQUE.RIVAS@LUZ.COM

Selected Clients
- Abbott Laboratories
- Alcon Laboratories
- Johnson & Johnson
- Life Technologies
- Novartis AG
- Stryker Corporation
- Smith & Nephew
- Siemens Medical Solutions

Project Specialization
- PC/Mac software globalization
- Web site globalization
- Product documentation/instructions

Industry Specialization
- Medical device/pharma

What languages do you expect to add over the next 12 months?
We anticipate adding support for more Indian and African languages for support

of global clinical trials.

Which translation software platforms do you support?

SDL Trados, SDL WorldServer, AURORA LSM platform (internal)

What percentage of your translation is currently performed "in the cloud"?

Very little is performed in what I would call the "commercial" cloud (e.g., Google) because it really does not apply to our vertical (life sciences). However, quite a bit of our actual translation work is performed through real-time TMS (WorldServer, AURORA, etc.)

Does your firm have any unique capabilities to add?

We are ISO 9001:2008 and ISO 13485:2003 certified. We also provide a suite of services that are unique to life science companies, such as linguistic validation of patient reported outcomes (PROs), IRAP Lite third-party reviews for reduced product liability, internal TMS with life science specific capabilities (AURORA LSM), etc.

What are the hottest industry trends that you are noticing now?

Structured authoring, maturation of translation purchasing processes for Fortune 1000 clients, and TM sharing (this has been a "hot topic" for several years now, it seems!).

What sets your agency apart from others?

We are life science specific. One hundred percent of our business and services offerings are for life science companies. If it is not life science–related and we can't do a good job of it, we don't take on the work.

MAGNUS

www.magnuscorp.com

FOUNDED IN:	1993
EMPLOYEES:	9 (70 FREELANCERS)
LANGUAGES:	150
HEADQUARTERS:	WALNUT, CA, USA
SALES CONTACT:	RICHARD ANTOINE 800-965-9321, EXT. 6111
	RANTOINE@MAGNUSCORP.COM

Selected Clients
- Anthem/Wellpoint
- United Healthcare
- Delta Dental
- Liberty Dental Plan

Project Specialization
- US healthcare market—translation of written materials for multiple media (web, print, broadcast)
- A/V services
- Interpreting—both telephonic and F2F, consulting in the areas of compliance and cost control, linguistic assessment, and training

Industry Specialization
- Medical device/pharma
- Health care
- Marketing firms/advertising agencies

Which translation software platforms do you support?
SDL Trados

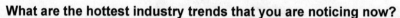

What are the hottest industry trends that you are noticing now?

Cost reduction efforts with an acceptance (or ignorance) of impacts on quality, which seems more a result of the economy and reduced staffing; and that many clients are becoming familiar with the term "translation memory" but very, very few truly understand it (or want to).

What sets your agency apart from others?

We have a laser-like focus on the US healthcare marketplace. We have extensive experience with regulatory oversight bodies, at both the federal and state levels, as well as an in-depth understanding of target consumers in various health insurance markets, both by product line and geographic location.

What advice would you give a company that is looking for a new translation vendor?

Ensure that the linguist team will be stable. Some companies use their "first string" linguists to get the work, then switch the work to others once they have the account.

Matrix Communications

www.matrix-ag.com

FOUNDED IN:	2006
EMPLOYEES:	30 (600 FREELANCERS)
LANGUAGES:	50+
HEADQUARTERS:	MUNICH, GERMANY
ADDITIONAL OFFICES:	MILAN, ITALY; TILBURG, THE NETHERLANDS; BRUSSELS, BELGIUM (JOINT VENTURE); SHEFFIELD, UK (JOINT VENTURE); BERLIN, GERMANY (JOINT VENTURE)
SALES CONTACT:	CHRISTIAN TAUBE +49 89 2000037 17 CHRISTIAN.TAUBE@MATRIX-AG.COM

Selected Clients
- European Union
- MAN Nutzfahrzeuge AG
- Munich Re
- NERO AG
- Royal Haskoning
- Santander Consumer Bank AG

Project Specialization
- Web site globalization
- Marketing collateral
- Product documentation/instructions

Industry Specialization
- Automotive
- Software
- Financial

What languages do you expect to add over the next 12 months?

More East Asian languages in terms of volume (we already have a significant share of revenues there but expect that to increase).

Which translation software platforms do you support?

SDL Trados, Google Translator Toolkit, GlobalSight, Across Language Server, WorldServer, Kilgray TMX Repository (Beta Programme), OmegaT, STAR Transit

Do you support machine translation? If so, what software do you use?

Yes: We currently partner with CrossLanguage in Brussels to set up MT projects in a hybrid approach (both rule-based and statistical) for specific projects.

Multimedia Languages & Marketing

www.2m.com.au

FOUNDED IN:	1999
EMPLOYEES:	3-5 (1,300 FREELANCERS)
LANGUAGES:	140
HEADQUARTERS:	BRISBANE, AUSTRALIA
ADDITIONAL OFFICES:	MELBOURNE AND PERTH
SALES CONTACT:	TEA DIETTERICH +61733678722
	MULTIMEDIA@2M.COM.AU

Selected Clients
- Australian Department of Foreign Affairs
- Australian Department of Trade & Commerce
- Australian Taxation Office
- Qld Department of Health
- Rio Tinto
- Australian Department of Immigration & Citizenship
- Brambles

Project Specialization
- Marketing collateral
- Product documentation/instructions
- Audio/Video localization/dubbing

Industry Specialization
- Consumer goods/retail
- Legal
- Marketing firms/advertising agencies

What languages do you expect to add over the next 12 months?
More African languages and indigenous languages.

Which translation software platforms do you support?
SDL Trados, Google Translator Toolkit

Do you support machine translation? If so, what software do you use?
Not much yet, but some of our translators use machine translation with extensive post editing, followed by checking by a second independent translator.

Does your firm have any unique capabilities to add?
Cross-cultural training, simultaneous interpreting, state-of-the-art dubbing, indigenous languages (rare African/Asian languages). We also provide text copywriting by international media journalists and authors.

What are the hottest industry trends that you are noticing now?
In Australia, the need for "emerging languages" due to refugee streams (i.e., rare African and Asian languages).

What sets your agency apart from others?
Company director Tea Dietterich is also National Vice President of AUSIT (Australian Institute of Interpreters & Translators) and therefore has a profound knowledge of the industry and her colleagues.

What advice would you give a company that is looking for a new translation vendor?
Check what is included in the price as you compare vendors—for example, our prices include translation by accredited translator, checking by a second independent translator, and proofing by an editor.

Net-Translators

www.net-translators.com

FOUNDED IN:	2002
EMPLOYEES:	60 (480 FREELANCERS)
LANGUAGES:	60+
HEADQUARTERS:	SUNNYVALE, CA, USA
SALES CONTACT:	SHY AVNI 408-501-8836
	SALESUSA@NET-TRANSLATORS.COM

Selected Clients
- Symantec
- Medtronic
- Adobe
- GE Healthcare
- NetApp
- Informatica
- Johnson & Johnson

Project Specialization
- PC/Mac software globalization
- Mobile app globalization
- Web site globalization

Industry Specialization
- Automotive
- Medical device/pharma
- Software/Hardware

Which translation software platforms do you support?
SDL Trados, Passolo, Catalyst

Does your firm have any unique capabilities to add?

We have a multilingual testing center with 32 languages supported in-house. Another added value is with the bidi languages, as our production is in Israel.

New Market Translations

www.nmtrans.com

FOUNDED IN:	2004
EMPLOYEES:	3 (384 FREELANCERS)
LANGUAGES:	40+
HEADQUARTERS:	MORRISTOWN, NJ, USA
SALES CONTACT:	MICHAEL MARSAN 973-796-2842
	MICHAEL.MARSAN@NMTRANS.COM

Selected Clients
- Microsoft
- Telcordia Technologies
- Amano
- Investors Savings Bank
- Globecomm
- Novartis
- Roche

Project Specialization
- Web site globalization
- Marketing collateral
- Product documentation/instructions

Industry Specialization
- Telecommunications
- Industrial/heavy equipment
- Health care

Which translation software platforms do you support?
Lionbridge Translation Workspace, WorldServer

What percentage of your translation is currently performed "in the cloud"?

100% (Our linguists have the option to work online or offline.)

What are the hottest industry trends that you are noticing now?

There are some serious quality issues with shared TMs that still require significant attention before we should consider them a hot trend. They are hot in terms of newsworthiness but not very practical at the moment. However, I do believe that shared TMs and machine translation will be common factors in the translation industry in the very near term. One of the hottest trends now is "hands-free" translation ecommerce, i.e., the elimination of person-to-person that is typically required to commence a translation project via translation ecommerce portals.

What sets your agency apart from others?

We provide consulting services to help enterprise clients set up in-house translation management capabilities.

One Hour Translation

www.onehourtranslation.com

FOUNDED IN:	2008
EMPLOYEES:	12 (8,000 FREELANCERS)
LANGUAGES:	51
HEADQUARTERS:	CYPRUS
ADDITIONAL OFFICE:	NEW YORK CITY
SALES CONTACT:	LIOR LIBMAN 954-396-5402
	LIOR@ONEHOURTRANSLATION.COM

Selected Clients
- IBM
- Pfizer
- McCann Erickson
- MorningStar
- Google
- Blinck
- Zynga

Project Specialization
High volume fast turnaround translations

Industry Specialization
- Software
- Financial
- Spanish for US localization

Which translation software platforms do you support?
SDL Trados, GlobalSight; in house XML/HTML editor

What percentage of your translation is currently performed "in the cloud"?

100%

Does your firm have any unique capabilities to add?

We are a 100% web-based professional translation service with more than 8,000 translators. We provide human translation API, professional translation plugins for several CMS, and email translation service—TransBox.

What are the hottest industry trends that you are noticing now?

Huge increase in demand for API services and automation of the translation submission retrieval and management processes.

What sets your agency apart from others?

Being web based, with very strong technological tools (API, TransBox, human translation plugins for CMS), and having translators with 24/7 service and availability.

PTIGlobal

www.ptiglobal.com

FOUNDED IN:	1977
EMPLOYEES:	45 (300 FREELANCERS)
LANGUAGES:	76
HEADQUARTERS:	BEAVERTON, OR, USA
SALES CONTACT:	JEFF WILLIAMS 888-357-3125
	JWILLIAMS@PTIGLOBAL.COM

Selected Clients
- Nvidia
- Warn Industries
- Gartner
- Intel
- Nike
- Rainbird
- Autodesk

Project Specialization
- PC/Mac software globalization
- Web site globalization
- Marketing collateral

Industry Specialization
- Medical device/pharma
- Software
- Marketing firms/advertising agencies

Which translation software platforms do you support?
SDL Trados, Passolo

Does your firm have any unique capabilities to add?

We have a large Managed Services Division consisting of translators, QA engineers, DTP specialists, technical writers, and project managers. This allows us to ramp up and down quickly for any given project in more than 30 languages on a daily basis.

What are the hottest industry trends that you are noticing now?

SaaS—Software as a Service

What mistakes do companies make when selecting translation vendors?

The number-one error is to assume that all companies are the same and are offering similar services at a comparative price. This is almost never the case. The other issue facing the industry is the view of translation and localization services as a commodity. The industry is dependent upon the services of actual people, and to view the service as a commodity does a disservice to the skills of the workforce.

Schreiber Translations, Inc. (STI)

www.schreibernet.com

FOUNDED IN:	1984
EMPLOYEES:	17 (800 FREELANCERS)
LANGUAGES:	100+
HEADQUARTERS:	ROCKVILLE, MD, USA
SALES CONTACT:	DAVID EVSEEFF 301-424-7737, EXT 125
	TRANSLATION@SCHREIBERNET.COM

Selected Clients
- SSA
- VA
- USPTO
- State of Maryland
- McAfee
- Lockheed Martin
- Raytheon

Project Specialization
- Web site globalization
- Marketing collateral
- Product documentation/instructions

Industry Specialization
- Medical device/pharma
- Legal
- Health care

What languages do you expect to add over the next 12 months?

We hope to add more exotic language capacity, such as Tongan, Samoan, and Marshallese.

Which translation software platforms do you support?

SDL Trados, Wordfast, Déjà Vu

What are the hottest industry trends that you are noticing now?

Hybrid machine translation

SDL

www.sdl.com

FOUNDED IN:	1992
EMPLOYEES:	2,112 (10,000 FREELANCERS)
LANGUAGES:	175
HEADQUARTERS:	MAIDENHEAD, UK
ADDITIONAL OFFICES:	60 LOCATIONS AROUND THE WORLD
SALES CONTACT:	EUROPE: +44 0 1628 410100
	USA: 303-440-0909
	GERMANY: +49 0 711 780 60

Selected Clients
- ○ ABN-Amro
- ○ Bosch
- ○ Microsoft
- ○ Philips
- ○ SAP
- ○ GlaxoSmithKline
- ○ Virgin Atlantic

Project Specialization
- ○ PC/Mac software globalization
- ○ Web site globalization
- ○ Product documentation/instructions

Industry Specialization
- ○ Automotive
- ○ Medical device/pharma
- ○ Software

Which translation software platforms do you support?
SDL Trados

What % of your translation is currently performed "in the cloud"?
90%, in our own private cloud

Do you support machine translation? If so, with what software?
Yes: SDL Language Weaver, SDL Enterprise Translation Server

What are the hottest industry trends that you are noticing now?
We are seeing an increasing interest in crowdsourcing, the cloud, and machine translation.

What sets your agency apart from others?
Our enterprise-level language solutions integrate into our complete global information management strategy to streamline the management process for the entire global content lifecycle.

As a leading language service provider, we operate an internal resource model employing more than 800 in-country translators in more than 60 global offices. This internal model tightly controls content quality and consistency, with all processes being supported by ISO 9001:2008 and EN 15038:2006 accreditation.

We also lead the way in integrating the latest technological innovations into our language services processes. Our recent acquisition of Language Weaver demonstrates an ongoing commitment to utilizing technology to further reduce costs and time-to-market for its blue-chip client base.

What mistakes do companies make when selecting translation vendors?
By not centralizing translation assets, companies are missing out on the cost and time benefits that come from re-using translated content across multiple departments and business units. By centralizing translation processes, companies can also adopt a unified quality control system for global deployment.

Syzygy Information Services

www.syzygy.com.tw

FOUNDED IN:	1997
EMPLOYEES:	27 (45 FREELANCERS)
LANGUAGES:	CHINESE (SIMPLIFIED, TRADITIONAL), JAPANESE, KOREAN, THAI, VIETNAMESE
HEADQUARTERS:	TAIPEI, TAIWAN
ADDITIONAL OFFICES:	HUA-LIAN, TAIWAN; AND MADRID, SPAIN
SALES CONTACT:	STEPHEN LEE +886 2 25621662 STEPHEN@SYZYGY.COM.TW

Selected Clients
- Microsoft
- Oracle
- Google
- McDonald's
- Logitech
- Moravia IT
- Welocalize

Project Specialization
- PC/Mac software globalization
- Mobile app globalization
- Web site globalization

Industry Specialization
- Software
- Computers and peripherals
- Health care

Which translation software platforms do you support?

SDL Trados, Google Translator Toolkit, GlobalSight, WorldServer

What percentage of your translation is currently performed "in the cloud"?

Less than 5%

What are the hottest industry trends that you are noticing now?

Request for online (web-based) translations.

TransAction Translators

www.transaction.co.uk

FOUNDED IN:	1983
EMPLOYEES:	4 (70+ FREELANCERS)
LANGUAGES:	38, WITH SPECIALIZATION IN DANISH, DUTCH, ENGLISH, FRENCH, GERMAN, ITALIAN, NORWEGIAN, SPANISH, SWEDISH
HEADQUARTERS:	SHEFFIELD, UK
SALES CONTACT:	ANNIKA VALE +44 114 266 1103
	TRANSACTION@TRANSACTION.CO.UK

Selected Clients
- Telefonica O2 Europe
- WHSmith Travel Retail
- Digital Control Inc
- Designflooring International
- HSBC Trust Company
- Swann Morton
- Siemens VAI

Project Specialization
- Web site globalization
- Product documentation/instructions
- Certified and legal official translations

Industry Specialization
- Automotive
- Legal
- Industrial/heavy equipment

Which translation software platforms do you support?
Déjà Vu X

Does your firm have any unique capabilities to add?
Being from Sheffield, steel and manufacturing.

What are the hottest industry trends that you are noticing now?
Web site localization and certified translations.

What sets your agency apart from others?
All projects are managed solely by qualified polyglot linguists. We have been full members of the Association of Translation Companies (ATC), UK, for more than 20 years.

What advice would you give a company that is looking for a new translation vendor?
Check for registration with a professional body such as the ATA or ATC; ask about their quality standards; ask for test translations; and ask if the projects are managed by linguists.

Translation Plus

www.translationplus.com

FOUNDED IN:	2000
EMPLOYEES:	8 (2,950 FREELANCERS)
LANGUAGES:	150
HEADQUARTERS:	HACKENSACK, NJ, USA
SALES CONTACT:	CARMEN ESTRADA 201-487-8007, EXT. 303
	CARMEN@TRANSLATIONPLUS.COM

Selected Clients
- UNDP
- Merck
- Genentech
- State of New Jersey
- University of Medicine and Dentistry of NJ
- UNICEF
- Barney's New York

Project Specialization
- Marketing collateral
- Product documentation/instructions
- Audio/Video localization/dubbing

Industry Specialization
- Medical device/pharma
- Health care
- Marketing firms/advertising agencies

Which translation software platforms do you support?
SDL Trados; evaluating XTM Suite and Lionbridge Translation Workspace

Does your firm have any unique capabilities to add?

Our Intercultural Advantage is a proprietary process that we use to insure that our translations reach the target ethnic audience as effectively as the source language material reaches its target audience.

What are the hottest industry trends that you are noticing now?

Sophisticated buyers are controlling their translation memory, enabling small translation companies with special capabilities to be seamlessly included in an overall corporate language solutions infrastructure.

What advice would you give a company that is looking for a new translation vendor?

Make sure that you have control of your translation memory. This creates a level playing field and allows you to obtain the pricing, delivery, and quality benefits that result from a small group of qualified vendors competing with one another for your business.

TransPerfect Translations International

www.transperfect.com

FOUNDED IN:	1992
EMPLOYEES:	1,400 (5,000+ FREELANCERS)
LANGUAGES:	100+
HEADQUARTERS:	NEW YORK CITY
ADDITIONAL OFFICES:	66 OFFICES IN THE US, EUROPE, ASIA, LATIN AMERICA, AND THE MIDDLE EAST
SALES CONTACT:	LISA CHAN 202-347-2300 LCHAN@TRANSPERFECT.COM

Selected Clients

- Apple
- General Electric
- Johnson & Johnson
- Marriott
- Nestle
- Sony
- UPS

Project Specialization

- PC/Mac software globalization
- Mobile app globalization
- Web site globalization

Industry Specialization

- Automotive
- Medical device/pharma
- Software

Which translation software platforms do you support?

Wordfast and all major TM tools.

What % of your translation is currently performed "in the cloud"?

TransPerfect uses its internally developed globalization management system, GlobalLink, to manage the majority of translation tasks in the cloud, and client review also takes place in the cloud. We estimate that 70% of all our translations are completed in a confidential cloud-based computing environment.

Does your firm have any unique capabilities to add?

GlobalLink Localization Suite is a modular group of technology applications designed to streamline every facet of the localization process. Each product can function independently or as part of an integrated, end-to-end solution. Alchemy is the leader in visual translation memory and provides a method for many of today's leading software companies to automate their build process. ABREVE is our authoring solution, designed to reduce and optimize source content for maximum re-use, and can help clients with appropriate content achieve a 20-40% reduction in overall translation spending.

What are the hottest industry trends that you are noticing now?

Desktop translation memory to server-based translation memory, greater use of translation workflow technology, off-shoring for low-cost testing and DTP services, source-content optimization, clients' desire for greater transparency into the translation process, vendor-neutral (vs. captive) technology products, increased emphasis on financial stability in the LSP selection process, and an increased acceptance of hosted turn-key technology solutions for web site localization.

What sets your agency apart from others?

We are the only major language services provider fully certified to the ISO 9001:2008 standard in all production centers worldwide. We were also the first major translation company to earn EN 15038:2006 certification, the only standard specifically created to address quality assurance practices for the translation industry.

TripleInk

www.tripleink.com

FOUNDED IN:	1991
EMPLOYEES:	10 (150-200) FREELANCERS
LANGUAGES:	40+
HEADQUARTERS:	MINNEAPOLIS, MN, USA
SALES CONTACT:	CHRISTA TIEFENBACHER-HUDSON 612-342-9790
	CTHUDSON@TRIPLEINK.COM

Selected Clients
○ BBDO
○ Business Incentives
○ Cardiac Concepts
○ Imris
○ Pfizer
○ St. Jude Medical
○ TBWA
○ TCF Bank

Project Specialization
○ Web site globalization
○ Marketing collateral
○ Transcreation

Industry Specialization
○ Medical device/pharma
○ Consumer goods/retail
○ Financial

What languages do you expect to add over the next 12 months?
Indian languages

Which translation software platforms do you support?
SDL Trados

Does your firm have any unique capabilities to add?
Our understanding of and experience in cross-cultural marketing informs our translation and transcreation work. It also enables us to provide consulting and creative services in the area of multicultural marketing and branding.

What are the hottest industry trends that you are noticing now?
"Transcreation" (which we have been practicing for the last nineteen years) seems to generating buzz.

What sets your agency apart from others?
Since our founding, our focus has been on translation in marketing and advertising. Our client services team includes cross-cultural marketing and communication professionals, and we have access to the creative and production resources of our parent company.

Welocalize

www.welocalize.com

FOUNDED IN:	1997
EMPLOYEES:	395 (700 FREELANCERS)
LANGUAGES:	107, WITH SPECIALIZATION IN JAPANESE, FRENCH (FRANCE), AND GERMAN (GERMANY)
HEADQUARTERS:	FREDERICK, MD
ADDITIONAL OFFICES:	BEIJING AND JINAN, CHINA; DUBLIN, IRELAND; SAARBRUCKEN, GERMANY; TOKYO, JAPAN; SEATTLE, WA; PORTLAND, OR; REDWOOD SHORES, CA
SALES CONTACT:	ERIN WYNN 480-575-5527
	ERIN.WYNN@WELOCALIZE.COM

Selected Clients
- Google
- Microsoft Corporation
- Apple
- Dell, Inc.
- Expedia, Inc.
- NetApp
- Canon Europe, Ltd.

Project Specialization
- PC/Mac software globalization
- Web site globalization
- Marketing collateral

Industry Specialization
- Software
- Consumer goods/retail

o Industrial/heavy equipment

Which translation software platforms do you support?

SDL Trados, Google Translator Toolkit, GlobalSight

What percentage of your translation is currently performed "in the cloud"?

Our GlobalSight SaaS solution is delivered through the cloud and accounts for approximately 30% of our translated content.

Do you support machine translation? If so, what software do you use?

GlobalSight supports MT automation with Google, Microsoft Translator, ProMT, Asia Online, and Moses.

Does your firm have any unique capabilities to add?

We have an "always-on" on-demand translation philosophy in order to keep up with the increased pace and volume of content demanded by end-users. Our efforts toward interoperability, extensibility, and standard data exchange across systems in the supply chain becomes essential to achieve the necessary reporting requirements and on-demand velocity.

What are the hottest industry trends that you are noticing now?

Sharing of translation memory, such as the TDA super cloud of translation memory data; on-demand translation with very short turnaround time; use of machine translation, and translation tool vendors working together to improve interoperability.

Wordbank Limited

www.wordbank.com

FOUNDED IN:	1988
EMPLOYEES:	76 (3,450 FREELANCERS)
LANGUAGES:	150
HEADQUARTERS:	LONDON, UK
ADDITIONAL OFFICE:	DENVER, CO
SALES CONTACT:	BRIAN GREGORY 720-359-1578
	BRIAN_GREGORY@WORDBANK.COM

Selected Clients
- Autodesk
- Deutsche Bank
- Hewlett-Packard
- Mazda
- Nike
- Towers Watson
- Walt Disney Company

Project Specialization
- Web site globalization
- Marketing collateral
- Audio/Video localization/dubbing

Industry Specialization
- Consumer goods/retail
- Marketing firms/advertising agencies
- Travel and Entertainment

What languages do you expect to add over the next 12 months?
We are increasingly dealing with less common languages such Xhosa, Nepalese,

Luxembourgish, Uzbek, Kazak, and Icelandic.

Which translation software platforms do you support?
SDL Trados, Wordbee Translator

Does your firm have any unique capabilities to add?
Search marketing translation—localizing all components of search marketing both paid and organic. This includes local keyword research, local web page optimization, AdWords transcreation, and landing page adaptation and testing. Also, advertising transcreation—transcreation and development of online and offline ads to ensure maximum effect in the local market.

What are the hottest industry trends that you are noticing now?
Everything is online, Dramatic increase in multimedia, continued reduction in the street price of "translation" due to the recession, and "free" translation.

What sets your agency apart from others?
We invest in long-term relationships—70% of our clients have worked with us for three years or longer. Eighty percent of our staff are fluent in three or more languages, and we were first certified in ISO 9001:2008 in 2003.

World Language Communications

www.worldlanguagecommunications.com

FOUNDED IN:	2007
EMPLOYEES:	5 (50 FREELANCERS)
LANGUAGES:	ALL LANGUAGES, WITH SPECIALIZATION IN SPANISH, PORTUGUESE, FRENCH, GERMAN, CHINESE, VIETNAMESE, KOREAN
HEADQUARTERS:	LOS ANGELES, CA, USA
SALES CONTACT:	ELENA HERNANDEZ 800-920-4816
	ELENA@WORLDLANGUAGECOMMUNICATIONS.COM

Selected Clients
- Siemens
- United Guaranty
- American Homeopathic Society
- Sherwin Williams
- Exclusive Visas
- Law Office of Angeline Chen
- Law Office of Mina Tran

Project Specialization
- PC/Mac software globalization
- Web site globalization
- Marketing collateral

Industry Specialization
- Medical device/pharma
- Financial
- Legal

What languages do you expect to add over the next 12 months?

Arabic, Hindi, Thai, Russian

Which translation software platforms do you support?

SDL Trados, Google Translator Toolkit

What percentage of your translation is currently performed "in the cloud"?

60%

Does your firm have any unique capabilities to add?

We have a large database of translators with high-level government clearances for work such as wire taps.

What are the hottest industry trends that you are noticing now?

Clients translating documents themselves with machine translations and asking us to have our editors fix the language. It is often more work than translating it from scratch, but most companies don't seem to understand that. I don't believe machine translation is at the level yet that it is 100% consistently cost effective to do that. Also, companies that would not have done so in the past are now creating entire divisions dedicated to translations so they can have them on salary for a fraction of the normal agency and freelance rates.

Additional Resources

Globalization Checklist

Here is a consolidated checklist of the many elements to keep in mind when taking software products and web content global. While this list may be overkill for localizing a marketing brochure, it is still worth skimming.

Preparation

- Assess your company's global readiness.
- Evaluate your target markets and locales. Ask the in-country teams for market-specific requirements.
- Test the effectiveness of your company and brand names in these new markets, or create new ones.
- For web sites, register country-code domain names.
- Evaluate the "world readiness" of your content and/or web site/ software application. Determine if internationalization should be handled in-house or outsourced to a vendor.

Internationalization

- Remove embedded text from images. Use culturally neutral images whenever possible.
- Test stability and flexibility of web sites/software by inserting different languages/scripts. Look for string concatenation.
  - Provide developers with guidelines for handling text expansion for buttons and legibility for Asian scripts.
- Develop support for local date/time formats, measurements, currency, mailing, and other region-specific features and content.
- Ensure that the software/web site supports Unicode encoding and any necessary encoding conversions.

Localization

- o Define the scope of your project, including the number of words and images requiring localization.
- o Estimate and allocate your budget. Set the schedule.
- o Develop your agency RFP. Select your vendor.
- o Prepare your source files, such as text, graphics, and scripts. Build a terminology glossary. Prepare detailed instructions for the translators.
- o Implement translation memory software.
- o Develop style guide.
- o Begin localization:
  - Translation
  - Editing
  - Graphics and design localization
  - In-country reviews

Maintenance and evolution

- o Train in-country staff to support content and customers.
- o Localization maintenance:
  - New source content must be localized
  - Changes to existing content must be reflected on all localized sites
  - Support customers via all channels, including phone, email, and in-store
  - Promote localized sites with advertising, PR, and search (SEO/SEM) initiatives

Review

- o Analyze web traffic, leads, sales by market.
- o Conduct quality audits of the translation(s).

Terminology

There are a lot of confusing terms used in the globalization industry, and it often seems that everyone within the industry has a slightly different definition. Here is how I define the following terms:

Back-translation

Hiring another translator or translation agency to tell you what your translated text is saying. This step is sometimes used by companies as a method of auditing the quality of their translation.

Bidirectional language (bidi)

Text that flows in both directions, such as Arabic and Hebrew, in which Latin-based numerals and words are read from left to right and the Arabic or Hebrew text is read from right to left.

CAT (computer-aided translation)

A broad term that may include a wide range of software tools designed to help translators work more quickly and/or improve the quality of their work. CAT tools range from electronic bilingual dictionaries to translation memory software.

Change order

When the scope of a translation or localization project changes or expands, an agency will issue a change order that the client must approve before the additional work can be completed. Change orders can quickly turn an on-time and under-budget project into a painful experience for both clients and agencies. The key to avoiding change orders is to work closely with your agency to minimize any last-minute changes or additions.

Country code

Two-digit codes, based on ISO 3166-1, used for representing a country or territory. These codes are largely used for country code Top Level Domains (ccTLDs), such as ".mx" for Mexico or ".fr" for France. A selected list of codes is located in the next section.

Domain name

A domain name is the unique alphanumeric text string that identifies a particular computer or domain (such as "amazon.com"). The domain name consists of two parts: the top-level domain (.com, .org, .fr, .cn) and second-level domain (amazon).

DTP

Acronym for *desktop publishing*.

F2F

Stands for *face to face*, a term used for interpreting services.

FIGS

An abbreviation frequently used in the translation industry to refer to French, Italian, German, and Spanish—the four major Western European languages.

Globalization

Globalization encompasses both the internationalization and localization of a web site or service. Because this term is so broad in nature, industry experts generally use the more narrowly defined terms: internationalization and localization.

Internationalization (i18n)

Internationalization, sometimes cryptically shortened to i18n, is the process of creating products and/or supporting materials so they can be easily localized. In web terms, the internationalization stage entails developing a global design template that works across all locales and making sure that all content and features are "world ready." The global gateway strategy and implementation falls under the internationalization process because it is foundational. The translation of individual language or country names may fall under the localization phase.

Internationalized domain name (IDN)

If any part of the domain name includes a non-ASCII character it is an Internationalized Domain Name (IDN). Although IDNs have been around for years, these are expected to go mainstream now that ccTLDs are receiving IDN counterparts. For example, there is .рф for .ru. For more information, visit http://www.globalbydesign.com/internationalized-domain-names.

Language code

Like country codes, there are also standard language codes. These are based on ISO 639-1 and you can learn more at http://en.wikipedia.org/wiki/List_of_ISO_639-1_codes. A selected list of codes appears in the next section.

Language pair

The combination of source language and target language, such as EN > FR (English translated into French). The arrow indicates the source and target languages. A translator will specialize in one language pair, typically his or her native language, and one additional language. The native language will usually be the target language.

L10n

The abbreviation for localization. The number refers to the number of letters between L and n.

Locale

A locale is a combination of language and region or country, such as French/Canada or English/UK. A number of attributes are often associated with a locale, such as time and date formats, currency, and measurements. The locale concept is valuable because it reinforces the notion that language and country may be related, but they are not equal. Language is typically a subset of location. By thinking in terms of locale, web developers can more effectively target users around the world.

Localization (L10n)

Localization, shortened to L10n, is the process of adapting products, software, or web sites for a specific locale. The process typically includes linguistic translation and technical and cultural modifications and adaptations. The more planning done at the internationalization stage, the easier the localization stage will be.

MLV (multi-language vendor)

A translation vendor who specializes in multiple language pairs, such as Western European languages.

Pseudolocalization

A process for testing the world-readiness of a software product or web site in which a mix of scripts are inserted in place of the source text to test how the product handles text expansion and display. The process is also valuable for identifying errant text strings that might have been left untranslated because they were isolated within the code.

SLV (single-language vendor)

A translation vendor who specializes in one language pair, such as English to/from Spanish.

Source language

The language one translates from. One may write the source and target pair as follows: English > French; this indicates English translated to French.

Splash page

A splash page, also known as a landing page, is a sort of "pre-home page" or "interstitial" that the web user sees before arriving at the formal home page. For years, companies used splash pages to promote new products or services—often with bandwidth-hogging animation. Thankfully, this practice has faded. But splash gateways have not gone away. They are now being used, quite productively, to allow web users to self-select their countries and/or languages.

Target language

The language one translates into. The source language is always positioned to the left side of notations such as: EN > FR or English > French.

Translation memory (TM)

The process and software tools that automate the re-use of previously translated terms and sentences. The larger a translation memory grows, the more valuable it generally becomes because it reduces the number of source words that require translation.

Translation vs. Transliteration

To translate text is to convey a similar message from one language to another language. But to transliterate is to convert text from one writing system into another writing system in a systematic way. The message is irrelevant; the goal is typically to convey a similar sound from one language to another. For example, Chinese city names have been romanized over the years. "Peking" was the result of an early form of transliteration; "Beijing" is based on a more recent romanization. For the purposes of this book, transliteration may be used when brand names are adapted to countries that use different writing systems. And this may carry over in the URL.

Unicode

Unicode is an international standard for representing the world's languages. Think of it as a super-sized alphabet that contains every character of every language. Most operating systems and applications support Unicode, and your web pages and applications should specify Unicode, specifically UTF-8. But keep in mind that not all computers have the necessary fonts to display all languages. To learn more, visit www.unicode.org.

Blogs, Twitter Feeds, and Additional Translation Resources

To help you cope with the information overload that is the Internet, here are some short lists of resources that I rely on to keep current on the industry.

Blogs I follow

Below is a selected list of blogs I follow. I also write a blog located at http://www.GlobalByDesign.com.

- Lionbridge Blog — http://blog.lionbridge.com/
- SDL Blog — http://blog.sdl.com/
- CSOFT Blog — http://blog.csoftintl.com/
- Adobe Globalization — http://blogs.adobe.com/globalization
- Google Translate — http://googletranslate.blogspot.com/
- Internet Stats Today — http://internetstatstoday.com/
- International Business Blog — http://globaledge.msu.edu/blog
- The Content Wrangler — http://thecontentwrangler.com/

Twitter feeds I follow

Below is a selected list of people I follow. For the complete list, visit my feed   @johnyunker.

- Adam Wooten — @AdamWooten
- BeatBabel — @BeatBabel
- Jack Waley-Cohen — @lingo24jwc

- ○ Kathleen Bostick   @KathleenBostick
- ○ Langology   @langology
- ○ Localization   @localization

Where to find additional translation agencies

Once you've worked your way through this directory, here are two other sources for finding agencies:

- ○ American Translators Association (www.atanet.org)
- ○ Proz (www.proz.com)

To hire freelance translators

Many smaller clients don't rely on translation agencies. Instead, they select and manage individual freelance translators themselves, as needed. But keep in mind that translation management can be very time consuming, particularly if numerous languages are involved. For example, a 5-language Web globalization project could easily involve 5 translators, 5 editors, and a few HTML production specialists—a lot of people to manage at once. To locate freelance translators, the resources mentioned above provide an excellent start.

To learn more about translation management

Below are some organizations, publications, and sources for additional training.

Organizations & Training

Society for Technical Communication (STC)

www. stc.org

The STC is an international organization for technical writers and managers. It includes a special interest group devoted to international communication issues. The member magazine, Intercom, also contains the occasional feature about translation and localization.

American Translators Association (ATA)

www.atanet.org

Although the ATA is an organization for translators, representatives of many major companies are members and will attend the annual conference. The ATA Web site is also a good place for learning more about the latest translation industry developments.

Localization Certification Program

California State University at Chico

Executive Certificate in Web Globalization Management

St. Louis University John Cook School of Business

Magazines/Newsletters

Multilingual Computing & Technology

www.multilingual.com

Multilingual Computing is an excellent magazine on translation, software localization, and web globalization. In addition, you can subscribe to their free newsletter.

The Translator's Tool Kit

www.internationalwriters.com/toolkit

A highly regarded biweekly technical newsletter for people in the translation industry.

Selected Country Codes

Here is a list of the more commonly used country codes, drawn from the ISO 3166 standard. A map of all ccTLDs is available at www.bytelevel. com/map.

.ae	United Arab Emirates	.ml	Mali
.ar	Argentina	.mx	Mexico
.at	Austria	.my	Malaysia
.au	Australia	.nl	Netherlands
.be	Belgium	.no	Norway
.br	Brazil	.nz	New Zealand
.ca	Canada	.pe	Peru
.ch	Switzerland	.ph	Philippines
.cl	Chile	.pl	Poland
.cn	China	.pr	Puerto Rico
.co	Colombia	.pt	Portugal
.cs	Serbia and Montenegro	.ro	Romania
.cz	Czech Republic	.ru	Russian Federation
.de	Germany	.sa	Saudi Arabia
.dk	Denmark	.sd	Sudan
.ec	Ecuador	.se	Sweden
.ee	Estonia	.sg	Singapore
.eg	Egypt	.si	Slovenia
.es	Spain	.sk	Slovak Republic
.eu	European Union	.th	Thailand
.fi	Finland	.tr	Turkey
.fr	France	.tv	Tuvalu
.gb	United Kingdom	.tw	Taiwan
.hk	Hong Kong	.tz	Tanzania
.hu	Hungary	.ua	Ukraine
.id	Indonesia	.uk	United Kingdom
.il	Israel	.us	United States
.in	India	.ve	Venezuela
.it	Italy	.vn	Vietnam
.jp	Japan	.yu	Yugoslavia
.kr	Korea, Republic of	.za	South Africa
.mk	Macedonia		

Selected Language Codes

Here is a list of the more commonly used two-digit language codes. These codes are part of the ISO 639 standard for the naming of languages. For the complete list, visit http://en.wikipedia.org/wiki/ISO_639.

Language	Code	Language	Code
Afrikaans	af	Macedonian	mk
Arabic	ar	Malay	ms
Armenian	hy	Malayalam	ml
Basque	eu	Marathi	mr
Bengali	bn	Norwegian	no
Bulgarian	bg	Oriya	or
Catalan	ca	Persian	fa
Chinese	zh	Polish	pl
Croatian	hr	Portuguese	pt
Czech	cs	Romanian	ro
Danish	da	Romansh	rm
Dutch	nl	Russian	ru
English	en	Serbian	sr
Estonian	et	Slovak	sk
Ewe	ee	Slovenian	sl
Finnish	fi	Spanish	es
French	fr	Swedish	sv
German	de	Tamil	ta
Greek	el	Telugu	te
Gujarati	gu	Thai	th
Hebrew	he	Turkish	tr
Hindi	hi	Ukrainian	uk
Hungarian	hu	Urdu	ur
Icelandic	is	Vietnamese	vi
Indonesian	id		
Italian	it		
Japanese	ja		
Kannada	kn		
Korean	ko		
Kurdish	ku		
Lao	lo		
Latvian	lv		
Luxembourgish	lb		

About the Author

John Yunker pioneered the development of best practices in global navigation and, over the years, he has helped hundreds of companies go global. John wrote the first book devoted to the emerging field of web globalization, *Beyond Borders: Web Globalization Strategies*. As co-founder of Byte Level Research, John has authored a number of landmark books and reports, including *The Web Globalization Report Card*, *Twittering in Tongues*, and *The Art of the Global Gateway*. For more information, visit www.bytelevel.com.

John also does corporate training and speaking, having spoken at industry events such as Internet Retailer, Localization World, and the Society for Technical Communication. He writes the popular blog Global by Design: www.globalbydesign.com.

Additional Products and Services

The 2010 Web Globalization Report Card

www.bytelevel.com/reportcard2010/

Tweeting in Tongues
How Companies are Going Global with Twitter

www.bytelevel.com/reports/twitter/

The Art of the Global Gateway
Strategies for Successful Multilingual Navigation

www.bytelevel.com/map/ccTLD.html

Country Codes of the World Map

www.bytelevel.com/map/ccTLD.html

Byte Level Research offers in-house web globalization and navigation training services. For more information, please visit us at www.
bytelevel.com/services.